First Edition

African Communities

An Inquiry Into The Theoretical Logic Of Community Formation

D1304094

By Thierno Thiam and Worth Kamili Hayes
Tuskegee University

Bassim Hamadeh, CEO and Publisher
Michael Simpson, Vice President of Acquisitions
Jamie Giganti, Managing Editor
Miguel Macias, Graphic Designer
Zina Craft, Acquisitions Editor
Monika Dziamka, Project Editor
Natalie Lakosil, Licensing Manager
Claire Yee, Interior Designer

First published in the United States of America in 2015 by Cognella, Inc.

Printed in the United States of America

ISBN: 978-1-63189-721-4/ 978-1-63189-722-1(br)

www.cognella.com   800-200-3908

This book is dedicated to
Aristotle Jones, Christian Felton, Jazlyn Fuller, Kierunya Davis,
Miriam Hammond, and Monyai Chavers.

Contents

List of Tables

List of Acronyms

AAFC:	Allied Armed Force of the Community
APRM:	African Peer Review Mechanism
AU:	African Union
ECOMOG :	Economic Community of West African States Monitoring Group
ECOWAS:	Economic Community of West African States
ECSC:	European Coal and Steel Community
EU:	European Union
FLS:	Front Line States
G8:	Group of Eight Leading Industrialized Nations
MERCOSUR:	Southern Common Market (Spanish: Mercado Común del Sur)
NAFTA:	North American Free Trade Agreement
NATO:	North Atlantic Treaty Organization
OAU:	Organization of African Unity
OPDS:	Organ on Politics, Defense and Security
PMDA:	Protocol on Mutual Defense Assistance
PSC:	Protocol Related to the Peace and Security Council
SADC:	Southern African Development Community
SADCC:	Southern African Development Coordination Conference
SCU:	Commissions and Sector Coordinating Units
SMC:	ECOWAS Standing Mediation Committee
SPA:	SADC Program of Action
UN:	United Nations

Abstract

As major paradigms of international politics, liberalism, constructivism and realism all prescribe solutions for the security dilemma. But, whereas liberalism and constructivism point to the development of communities, especially security communities, as a means to overcome the security dilemma, realism relies on power politics and interest. While liberalism points to shared values and constructivism to shared identity, realism points to shared interest. In this study, we use three African cases, notably the African Union (AU), the Economic Community of West African States (ECOWAS) and the Southern African Development Community (SADC), to test the explanatory power of these three paradigms. Our findings suggest that none of the paradigms provide a satisfactory explanation for the emergence of communities and security communities in Africa. Although liberalism and constructivism, in general, offer more elaborate theories of communities and security communities, their explanations for the emergence of the AU, ECOWAS and the SADC are faced with insurmountable obstacles. As for realism, although confronted with serious limitations, it constitutes a closer fit to all three African cases. Such a finding runs counter to the general literature about communities and security communities, which remains characterized by its Eurocentric approach.

Chapter 1

Introduction

D o the major paradigms of international politics explain the emergence of communities in Africa in general and security communities in particular? This is the central question this study seeks to answer. To address this critical question, this study will analyze Africa's integration experiments through its major regional organizations, notably the African Union (AU), the Economic Community of West African States (ECOWAS) and the Southern African Development Community (SADC). Most specifically, do liberalism, constructivism and realism tell us enough about the conditions under which communities and security communities develop in Africa? Do the universalistic claims of the major paradigms of international politics hold? In other words, do communities arise in similar conditions regardless of any other considerations?

In this respect, this study challenges the existing paradigms by putting them to the test of the emergence of the major communities in Africa in order to explore alternative ways of analyzing the conditions under which security communities develop. In a nutshell, the liberal paradigm is built around the hypothesis that common values (e.g., democratic values) lead to the emergence of communities. As for the constructivist paradigm, it is premised on the hypothesis that common identity constitutes a central prerequisite for the emergence of communities. Finally, the realist paradigm, especially in its neorealist version, is built around the notion that the rise of communities is essentially a function of structure. The following underlying questions are raised by the major assumptions of these different paradigms: (1) do they tell the whole story or (2) do the African cases call for a retesting of the main hypotheses of the existing paradigms or a testing of new ones?

In this study, we argue that none of these three major paradigms explains the emergence of communities and security communities in Africa. Although liberalism and constructivism offer more elaborate theories of the rise of communities and security communities, the three African cases, notably the AU, ECOWAS and the SADC, present them with obstacles that they cannot surmount. The realist paradigm, counterintuitively, provides a better explanation for the rise of communities and security communities in Africa. Realism, however, through its focus on the state as the unit of analysis, is faced with its own problems in explaining the African cases.

The major problem with all of these paradigms is that they leave out a key variable, notably individual leadership. As we shall show in this study, individual leadership constitutes perhaps the single most important variable in the rise of communities and security communities in Africa. Consequently, after laying out the problems with the existing paradigms, the final section of this study will be devoted to laying out an alternative explanation of the emergence of communities and security communities based on the variable of individual political leadership.

This research, which then proposes an alternative explanation to the emergence of communities in Africa based on political leadership, is informed by the broad scholarship on political leadership. Specifically, it draws on the conceptualization of the variable of political leadership in the African context. Such conceptualization is largely based on the inverse relationship between individual leadership and institutional design and is based on the notion that, in the absence of strong institutions, individual leaders in Africa tend to play an unusually crucial role (Jackson and Rosberg 1982). In this sense, this research does not intend to offer a detailed theory of political leadership. What it intends to do is indicate the ways in which the variable of political leadership has been central to understanding the process of security community building in Africa. Consequently, this research will posit the leadership variable as a fourth and more useful perspective from which the emergence of international and security communities can be understood. Broadly, leadership in this research will be understood in terms of the individual heads of state from the different African nations that were determinant in the creation of Africa's three communities.

The actions of these individual heads of state, we argue, although constrained more or less by institutional realities, remain the sine qua non in the rise of international and security communities in Africa. For all these reasons, Chapter 7, which is designed as an exploratory venue of the variable of political leadership as an alternative perspective for analyzing the rise of communities in Africa, will test two major hypotheses. Such hypotheses are derived from the variable of leadership. The first hypothesis is built around the notion that communities are more likely to emerge when a charismatic political leader is willing to be the driving force behind the organization. As for the second hypothesis, it is structured around the notion that communities are more likely to emerge when a charismatic political leader is willing to be the driving force behind the organization in the presence of favorable institutional factors.

I. Rationale

Our choice of this specific subject is justified by a variety of reasons. As major paradigms of international relations, liberalism, constructivism and realism all prescribe solutions for the security dilemma. But, whereas liberalism and constructivism point to the development of security communities as a means to overcome the security dilemma, realism relies on power politics in the formation of alliances. In this study, we use the African case in general, and the African Union, ECOWAS and the SADC in particular, in order to test these three paradigms.

In this respect, this study intends to focus on a part of the world that has been left at the margins of scientific enquiry among the major paradigms of international politics. This relative lack of interest in the African experience might be explained by the fact that, as Hans Morgenthau (1948, 27) contends, the immediate aim of international politics is power. In this respect, it is not surprising that Africa has been left out of the realm of the scientific enquiry precisely because it does not speak the language of power on the international stage. In this sense, the new international context, marked by the reemergence of regional integration as one of the most important developments of world politics (Mattli 1999, 189), makes a focus on the African experience in integration all the more relevant. Lessons from such experience could contribute something essential to the scholarship.

Finally, it is also important to note that security communities are theoretically interesting in the sense that the security aspect of international communities constitutes their most inclusive aspect. In other words, an analysis of the security aspect of international communities also takes into account the three major dimensions of such communities, notably economics, politics and security. This is all the more true since virtually all security communities have an economic and political component. Such economic and political components constitute the basis for the security mechanism of such communities. The three cases of this study (i.e., the AU, ECOWAS and the SADC) as well as the case of NATO, the world's foremost security community—in which the need for security arises out of the need to protect the economic, political and other kinds of interests of the member states—constitute the most potent illustrations to this point. In this respect, the emergence of a security community represents the most finite stage of the phenomenon of international integration.

On the other hand, all economic and political communities do not necessarily have a security component. The North American Free Trade Agreement (NAFTA) and the Southern Common Market, commonly referred to in Spanish as Mercado Común del Sur (MERCOSUR), may be the most salient examples of a community based solely on economic interests. In this sense our focus on security communities does not necessarily exclude economic and political considerations. For this reason, although the primary focus of this study will be on security communities, our analysis will also be informed by the economic and political underpinnings of such security communities.

All three African communities, notably the AU, ECOWAS and the SADC, are political, economic and security communities. The fact that these are political and economic communities is obvious. The less obvious and nonetheless true fact is that they are security communities. The reason for such ambiguity rests mainly on the fact that they do not fit the mold of a traditional security community like NATO, in the sense that they started as general political and economic communities and then evolved progressively into security communities. Such evolution will be discussed with each individual community.

At this point, it will suffice to point out that the issue surrounding the evolution of African communities from economic and political organizations into security communities has been settled by scholars of African politics such as Alhaji Bah (2005), Benedikt Franke (2008), Gina Schalkwyk (2005) and Maxi Schoeman (2002). Using all three African cases, Franke (2008), for instance, argues that the emergence of such communities could be best described by what he calls "multilayered security communities." In other words, he submits that while it is difficult to conceptualize Africa's security communities in much the same ways in which the traditional theoretical frameworks did with both NATO and the EU, the fact remains that Africa's communities are different kinds of security communities in which different states are members of more than one security community at the same time (Franke 2008, 314). Franke builds his argument both from the constructivists as well as the liberals to demonstrate that Africa's communities, notably the AU, ECOWAS and the SADC, can be considered as pluralistic security communities, in the sense that their evolution is consistent with the patterns of security communities and they display all the defining characteristics of security communities (Franke 2008, 239). Pluralistic communities stand in contrast with amalgamated communities. The main difference between the two resides in the fact that pluralistic communities constitute a much looser association. States that form pluralistic communities retain much of their sovereignties.

This study will focus on security communities in Africa. The notion of security communities has been conceptualized best by Karl Deutsch. According to Deutsch, the idea of security communities refers to the creation of conditions for a stable and peaceful relationship among different nations (Deutsch 1954, 33). In other words, security communities are international organizations created by different states aimed at providing protection from cross-national and/or internal war involving one or more parties.

II. Research Method

This study will consist of case studies of Africa's three major communities: the AU, ECOWAS and the SADC. Each of these three cases will be analyzed with a special focus on examining whether the conditions under which they emerged and evolved are consistent with the prescriptions of the three major international relations paradigms, notably liberalism, constructivism and realism.

To paraphrase Steven Van Evera (1997), this study will be conducted with the following question in mind: Do the events that lead to the advent of security communities in Africa unfold in the manner in which the major paradigms of international relations predict? Such question gives rise to at least two major scenarios.

The first one is that the emergence of Africa's three major communities is explained satisfactorily by one or more of the three major paradigms. Should this be the case, the study will elaborate on the merits of such paradigms. The second scenario is one in which none of the paradigms explains satisfactorily the emergence of Africa's communities. Should the answers provided by the major paradigms be unsatisfactory, this study will lay out the limitations of such paradigms in an attempt to generate new hypotheses that offer alternative ways of thinking about the conditions under which communities in general, and security communities in particular, develop. And, as in the case of this project, the exploration leads to an examination of the centrality of leadership as to the construction of African security communities. The findings below suggest the importance of leadership and the insufficiency of the three paradigms in addressing the issue of leadership.

The data for this research will be drawn from the official reports of the AU, ECOWAS and the SADC and from official reports from a variety of the member states as well as newspaper reports. This study will also draw from the previous research in the field of African politics, especially in its treatment of such integration mechanisms. We also intend to draw from the much larger international integration literature. Overall, the integration literature is characterized by an overarching emphasis on European integration (see Deutsch 1954; Deutsch et al. 1957; Risse-Kappen 1996; Rosamond 2000). Consequently, the paradigms that that are derived from such literature are built on assumptions about integration processes that are conceptually, geographically and historically bounded. This could explain why such literature has only considered the case of the recent development of the African Union as a mere aftershock of the development of the European Union. Thus, by ignoring the specificities of the African Union and other communities in Africa such as ECOWAS and the SADC, the literature is guilty of oversimplifying and overlooking major aspects of Africa's integration mechanisms. Analyzing Africa's case with new lenses has the potential to contribute something new to the literature. This is especially true since, as we have previously pointed out, although the issue of African integration has generated a significant amount of scholarship, such scholarship tends to focus primarily on ideological and practical policy issues, but most importantly on economic issues (Diop 1987; Nkrumah 1963; UNECA 2006; Clapham 2001; Collier and Venables 2008).

Methodologically, Africa's three major communities constitute interesting cases, especially in terms of their similarities and differences. They also exhibit similarities as well as differences with other major international communities such as the European Union (EU) and the North Atlantic Treaty Organization. For this reason, this study will also make use of the comparative historical analysis method. Most specifically, it will make use of what Theda Skocpol and Margaret Somers (1980) called the 'method of agreement,' which uses 'most similar cases,' and the 'method of disagreement,' which uses 'most different cases' for two essential reasons.

First, our three cases do allow for the use of the "most similar" comparison method in order to examine how similar causal mechanisms operate in different contexts to produce broadly similar patterns. These patterns lead to the emergence of communities in general and security communities in particular. Second, our three cases also allow for the use of the "most different" method in order to understand what is distinctive about each case and what distinguishes each case from other international cases such as the EU and NATO. Skocpol (1979, 40) argues that "comparative historical analysis works best when applied to a set of a few cases that share certain basic features." For Skocpol (1979, 36), the use of the "method of agreement" in conjunction with the "method of disagreement" constitutes one of the best ways to overcome the methodological issues that are related to small sample sizes and qualitative research in general. Whereas the "method of agreement" is used by comparing cases that are most similar and have in common both the phenomenon that one seeks to explain and the causal factors that lead to the phenomenon, the "method of disagreement" is used by contrasting "cases in which the phenomenon to be explained and the hypothesized causes are present to other cases in which the phenomenon and the causes are both absent, but which are otherwise as similar as possible to the positive cases" (Skocpol 1979, 36).

In our three cases, such similarities include the contexts in which all three communities developed. These similarities make a comparative study an ideal case scenario for understanding the causes that lead to their emergence. It is also important to recognize, however, that comparison as a method of political inquiry presupposes the existence of a system of controlling for other variables. This control plays a key role in diminishing the margins of errors in comparative studies by the mere assurance that the researcher could reasonably identify which factors cause which results if every other factor is held constant. This ceteris paribus condition is fundamental to any empiric generalization. In this respect, our three cases, which present differences in terms of their institutional evolution, could in fact serve that purpose. Therefore, it is only befitting that in addition to analyzing the similarities between our cases we will contrast them to determine the causal mechanisms that lead to the emergence of communities in general and security communities in particular. In addition, the analysis of the similarities and differences will also extend to other major international communities such as the EU and NATO.

Finally, this study will be organized in the following manner. Chapter 2 will consist of an overview of the major paradigms of international politics as they relate to international integration. The third chapter will analyze Africa's communities including both its earliest and modern communities. Africa's modern communities, notably the AU, ECOWAS and the SADC, which will be the focus of this study, are natural progressions from Africa's early communities. While not the central focus of this research, it is important to understand that traditions of trans-societal community building in Africa are as old as African societies. The fourth, fifth, and sixth chapters will examine the emergence of the AU, ECOWAS and SADC, respectively, in light of the paradigms of international politics. The seventh and final chapters will attempt to move beyond the existing paradigms and put forward new ways of explaining the emergence of communities, and especially security communities, in Africa.

III. Background

The emergence of the African Union has often been described as an event of immense magnitude in the institutional evolution of the African continent by most scholars and political analysts. This event, however, was preceded by the advent of two major regional communities: the Economic Community of West African States (ECOWAS) and the Southern African Development Community (SADC), formerly the Southern African Development Coordination Conference (SDCC), respectively in 1975 and 1980. The African Union itself emerged to replace a dysfunctional Organization of African Unity (OAU). As major integration organizations, all three communities (the AU, ECOWAS and the SADC) are characterized by a major security component in addition to a political and economic component.

The three communities epitomize the African experience in integration. Each of the three communities, however, emerged in similar yet very unique historical and institutional circumstances. The SADC, for instance, evolved from an anti-Apartheid community in 1980 to undergo a dramatic change in 1992 to include major security dispositions. As for ECOWAS, it started mainly as an economic community and grew into a security community in 1990 with the institution of the Economic Community of West African States Monitoring Group (ECOMOG), a West African multilateral armed force. The creation of ECOMOG was followed by major changes in the charter of ECOWAS, which sought to strengthen the security dispositions of the subregional organization. The case of the African Union is both unique and different from the two subregional organizations (i.e., ECOWAS and the SADC) in the sense that it took into account the evolutional patterns of both organizations as well as the mistakes of its predecessor, the OAU, in an attempt to be as comprehensive as possible. In this study, our focus will be on the security aspect of these three integration organizations.

The concept of integration in international politics has been defined in a variety of ways. Broadly, the concept of integration refers to a shift of sovereignty from state structures to regional structures. It is a process whereby a supranational institution supersedes and replaces the existing institutions of the member states of a given community. Such sovereignty shift could be in the form of a loose association in which the states that form the union retain the essence of their national sovereignties, as exemplified by the case of the European Union. The sovereignty shift could also be in the form of a tighter association in which the states delegate their national sovereignties to a federal system, such as the United States of America and Germany.

At the theoretical level, two major currents are discernible among the major scholars of integration. The first current, which is consistent with the realist paradigm, argues that communities become integrated in the presence of threat or force. Such a current, which is state-centered, draws its origins from Hobbes whose central argument rests upon the recognition of the function of coercion in the integration of political communities. This tradition is also enriched by the works of Johan Galtung. For Galtung (1968, 377), the concept of integration is defined as "the process whereby two or more actors form a new actor. When the process is completed, the actors are said to be integrated." Most importantly, Galtung distinguishes three kinds of integration: territorial, organizational and associational. For Galtung, these three forms are closely interrelated and are not mutually exclusive. However, whereas organizational integration and associational integration are more closely associated and complementary and always tend to satisfy some human needs, territorial integration depends very much on communication and tends to disappear with increasing communication.

The second and dominant current among integration theories, however, remains inspired by the liberal tradition and the paradigms that are also based on the rejection of realism as an organizing principle of international politics, notably constructivism and functionalism. Most specifically, these paradigms reject the analysis of Galtung and in general the neorealist's structural analysis, which takes the state as the dominant actor to the exclusion of every other non-state actor. Ernest Haas (1958, 16), for instance, defines integration as "the process whereby political actors in several distinct national settings are persuaded to shift their loyalties, expectations and political activities toward a new center, whose institutions possess or demand jurisdictions over preexisting national states." For Haas, this process inevitably results in the fact that a new community is superimposed over the preexisting ones. Building from the definition of Haas and using the case of the European Community, Leon Lindberg (1963, 6) contends that integration can be defined as "(1) the process whereby nations forgo the desire and ability to conduct foreign and key domestic policies independently of each other, seeking instead to make joint decisions or to delegate the decision-making process to new central organs; and (2) the process whereby political actors in several distinct settings are persuaded to shift their expectations of and political activities to a new center." As for Amitae Etzioni (1965, 329), who analyzes the concept of integration from a Weberian perspective, he argues that a political community is integrated when it possesses "(a) an effective control over the use of the means of violence, (b) has a center of decision-making that is able to affect significantly the allocation of resources and rewards throughout the community and (c) is the dominant focus of political identification for the large majority of politically aware citizens."

Karl Deutsch et al. (1957, 5), who are arguably the most influential theorists in this tradition, on the other hand, contend that the concept of integration in international relations could be understood in terms of the existence of social groups with a process of political communication, some machinery for enforcement and some popular habits of compliance. What differentiates Deutsch and his collaborators on one hand and other theorists of integration such as Haas, Galtung and even Joseph Nye on the other hand is that Deutsch primarily understands the concept of integration in terms of the rise of security communities within a region. In other words, whereas a significant number of integration theorists in the mold of Haas, Galtung and Nye posit a broader conceptualization of integration as a function of a variety of factors (including economics, politics and security), Deutsch's analysis of the concept of integration accords a central place primarily to the notion of security communities.

The concept of security community evokes the notion that the integration mechanism, which brings different nation-states and other actors together, takes place out of a concern for security and stability. Its origins can be traced back to the state of nature. When the French political philosopher Jean Jacques Rousseau (1755) argued in his seminal work that the solution to the Hobbesian state of nature is the social contract, whereby individuals form small communities, he was formulating the first theories of security communities.

The most systematic and rigorous theory of security communities, however, has been formulated by Deutsch. For Deutsch et al. (1957, 5), a security community can be defined as a group of people that has become integrated to the point that there is a "real assurance that the members of that community will not fight each other physically, but will settle their disputes in some other way." Equally important, and along the lines of general integration theories, Deutsch distinguishes two types of security communities: amalgamated communities and pluralistic communities. Whereas the first category is characterized by a fusion of the institutions of the member states, the second category is constituted of a looser association of the member states who retain their sovereignties. With respect to Africa, all of its three communities fall in the category of pluralistic communities since all three organizations remain committed to the sanctity of the sovereign territories of their member states. In this study, we will focus on analyzing the concept of integration through the emergence of communities in general and security communities in the particular case of Africa.

The concept of African integration, which has generated a considerable amount of literature, finds its deepest roots in the Pan-African movement (Nye 1965, 1). The origins of Pan-Africanism could be traced back to Africa's ancient communities. Political entities like Kanem (700 AD–1376 AD), Ghana (750 AD–1076 AD), Bachwezi (1200 AD–1300 AD), Mali (1235 AD–1645 AD), Jolof (1350–1890 AD) and Songhai (1375 AD–1591 AD) regrouped a variety of smaller entities and kingdoms under one centralized and amalgamated community. Thus while the Mali empire included much of today's West African states, the Bachwezi empire included much of Uganda, northern Tanzania and eastern Congo (DRC).

As a modern movement, however, Pan-Africanism was revived in the twentieth century by a group of scholars and politicians such as Edward W. Blyden, William E. B. Du Bois, Kwame Nkrumah and Gamal Abdel Nasser who sought to integrate both native Africans and the African diasporas into a unified African community. As we previously pointed out, the modern literature on African integration, born after the 1960s with the birth of most modern African states, has mainly focused on ideological and practical policy justifications related to the reasons Africa is in need of integration (Diop 1987; Nkrumah 1963). To date, a systematic theoretical approach, which draws from the theories of international integration in light of Africa's integration processes, is both timely and useful in the sense that it has the potential to contribute to our understanding of the crucial issue of political integration. Challenging major theories of international integration by using the African experience has the potential to allow for a reexamination of assumptions and therefore may contribute to strengthening such theories.

Chapter 2

An Overview of The Major Paradigms of International Politics

T he goal of this chapter is to examine integration theories as tools for understanding how and why states collaborate and build shared institutions. This chapter is motivated by the conviction that, as Milton Friedman (1953, 33) has suggested, "there is a way of looking at or interpreting or organizing the evidence that will reveal superficially disconnected and diverse phenomena to be manifestations of a more fundamental and relatively simple structure." In this spirit, this chapter will begin by providing a brief review of the integration literature in general. Secondly, it will focus on the major paradigms around which this study will be built, notably realism, liberalism and constructivism.

I. Why Do Communities Integrate?

Why do states decide to compromise their sovereignties in favor of a supranational entity? This question is at the heart of the integration literature and can be answered by considering a wide variety of perspectives including federalism, functionalism, collective goods, liberalism, constructivism, realism, etc. Because the liberal, constructivist and realist paradigms will be the focus of this study and have already been introduced, a brief overview of other major integration approaches may be called for. Such approaches will be discussed in this chapter to provide a reader with a broader perspective.

They will not, however, be discussed separately in the analytical sections of this study for two essential reasons. The first one is related to the fact that the central ideas they discuss can also be found in the three major paradigms on which this study will focus. Federalism is one example of this, as one of its main proponents, Jean Jacques Rousseau, can also be considered a key figure of early liberalism. The second reason is related to the fact that such approaches may have emerged to explain specific integration cases and do not lend themselves to the explanation of a universal phenomenon.

The functionalist approach, which will be discussed in this section, constitutes a prime example of this point in the sense that its explanation of the rise of the European Union is based on circumstances that are unique to the European experience and such experience is not replicable. Nevertheless, the influence of these three theoretical traditions on integration theories do grant them a place in this section—despite the limits in their explanatory power, their influence on the liberal, constructivist and realist tradition can never be overstated. Such influence can be seen, for instance, in the fact that some of the major proponents of these early traditions (federalism, functionalism and collective goods) also exercise a tremendous influence on the liberal, constructivist and realist paradigms. Among the most prominent examples are Rousseau who is considered both a federalist as well as a liberal and Deutsch who is often mentioned in functionalist discussions and considered a liberal as well.

Federalism is one of the very first approaches that attempted to explain systematically the phenomenon of international integration. Like most integration theories, the essence of federalism lies in its explanation of the transfer of sovereign authority from state institutions to a supranational institution. The federalist view is perhaps better understood through the contributions of the French political philosopher Jean Jacques Rousseau. In his defense of the concept of a united Europe, Rousseau (1761, 4) explains that in order for the states of Europe to escape the security dilemma, they had to invest their sovereignties into a federal entity. Rousseau's rationale is based on the fact that the insecurity of Europe in the eighteenth century was the direct product of the sovereign relations among different states and the solution to such a security dilemma rested with a voluntary association between the different states of Europe.

To make his case, Rousseau drew from the historic cases of the Amphictyonic League in ancient Greece which consisted of an association of neighboring states formed around a religious center; the Etruscan federation which was made up of twelve city-states; the Latin federation which included Crete, Venice, the Kingdom of Thessalonica, the Principality of Achaea, the Duchy of Athens, the Duchy of the Archipelago, etc.; and the Gallic empire which included the Roman provinces of Gaul, Britannia, Hispania and Baetica. According to Rousseau, these federations were designed to create a sense of security within the community of states that composed it. However, Rousseau claimed that the major federations which came after these primitive cases contained more wisdom than their predecessors, in the sense that they constituted improvements based on the lacunas of previous experiences. In this respect, he argues that the Germanic Body, the Helvetic League and the States General, for instance, were more perfect unions than their predecessors.

Functionalism constitutes yet another major approach to understanding international integration. Unlike, the federalist approach, the functionalist and neofunctionalist approaches contend that supranational structures are created out of the need for a group of states to seek practical means to fulfill specific functions such as delivering mail from one country to another. David Mitrany (1975), for instance, explains that the impact of modernization on world politics can be measured in terms of the myriad of problems that can best be resolved by experts as opposed to politicians. Such problems can be found within states as well as between states. The proliferation of these common problems logically requires collaborative responses from different states. In this respect, integration is a product of economic and technological development.

The underlying question that functionalism faces is, How do we explain the fact that European integration went beyond the need to fulfill some limited specialized functions and translated into a political development such as the European Union? For Mitrany (1975), the answer can be found in the fact that such collaboration in one or more technical or functional issues would lead to further collaboration in a variety of other areas. He calls the process ramification. In this respect, the political integration of Europe is the logical ramification of the creation of the European Coal and Steel Community (ECSC) in 1952. The technical and functional common issues that the original six members of the ECSC (France, Germany, Italy, Belgium, Holland and Luxembourg) faced in their attempt to maximize the benefits of exploiting their common coal and steel mines eventually called for a broader set of responses. These responses went beyond their original technical and functional intent in order to include a political component.

Ernest Haas' neofunctionalism goes one step further in its attempt to situate the importance of different actors in the process of integration. He recognizes the importance of national states but also stresses the roles of regional interest groups and the bureaucracy of regional organizations. In other words, although the member states create the initial conditions, regional interest groups and international bureaucrats push the process of integration forward, while national governments increasingly solve conflicts of interest by conferring more authority on the regional organizations as citizens increasingly look to the regional organization for solutions to their problems.

For Hass (1961), as a process, the concept of integration comports both an intellectual as well as a normative aspect. Intellectually, Haas' brand of neofunctionalism tries to correct functionalism's failure to explain how the integration process starts out of economic and technical concerns and extends to the political realm, as in the case of the evolution of the ECSC into the EU. Haas explains that economic integration creates political integration through a process of spillover. He calls this process the positive spillover effect. In other words, integration between states in one economic sector will quickly create strong incentives for integration in other sectors in order to fully capture the benefits of integration in the original sector. With respect to the normative aspect of integration, Hass argues that the result of integration processes is beneficial to the member states in the sense that regional entities are potential "islands of cooperation" that could constitute building blocks for world peace.

However, functionalism and neofunctionalism's lack of explanatory power in accounting for the universal phenomena is no longer a matter of debate. The obsolescence of the functionalist approach in explaining the rise of communities has been revealed by none other than one of its own major advocates, Ernest Haas (1975). The main reason for the lack of explanatory power of the functionalist approach resides in the fact that its explanation for the process of integration relies on a unique case with no universal applications. The case of the European Union as the grandchild of the ECSC is too singular to have any universal replications. If Haas' remarks bear any major implications, it is the fact that the experience of the original "six" founding members[1] in the integration of Europe is too singular to be reproducible. For this reason, the next sections of this study will not focus on the functionalist and neofunctionalist paradigms.

Finally, the collective goods approach also puts forth a persuasive account of the conditions under which international integration occurs. According to the collective goods perspective, communities emerge for a variety of reasons. Garrett Hardin's (1968) Tragedy of the Commons is located at the heart of the collective goods approach. Most specifically, the biologist, in his story of a group of herders who share a common grazing area and therefore a collective good, poses a problem that is similar to the dilemma which different states face in their international relations. In Hardin's cases, the dilemma can be measured by the fact that each herder finds it economically rational to increase the size of their herds because doing so translates into more revenue. However, if every herder follows the same course of action, then the group as a whole loses; seeking to maximize production will lead to more animals grazing the land resulting in lower quality pastures and a weaker output.

At the international level, the relations between sovereign nation-states are no different. The goal of each state is to maximize its power (power is understood in economic terms in this particular case) regardless of the impact of its actions on the international collective good. For Hardin, the solution to the collective goods problem could be twofold. Coercing or influencing state preferences may lead states to take action that will be favorable to the preservation of the collective good. In this sense, he argues that drastic actions may be needed both at the national and international level to force people and states to save the collective good. In his view, policies that force people to limit the number of children they have could be understood in such light. Second, at the international level, the policy of the stick and the carrot which aims at punishing a given state for a behavior which compromises the collective good and rewarding it for a behavior which enhances the collective good could provide a solution to the problem.

II. The Realist Paradigm

What does political realism contribute to our understanding of international integration? To tackle this question, our discussion of political realism will

---

1   Belgium, France, West Germany, Italy, Luxembourg and Netherlands.

focus on the three major variants of the realist paradigm, notably classical real-ism, post–World War realism and neorealism. As the earliest trend in realism, the essence of classical realism is captured best by the writings of scholars such as Thucydides, Niccolo Machiavelli and Thomas Hobbes. As for post–World War realism, it is best captured by the contributions of the major realists such as E. H. Carr and Hans Morgenthau. And finally, the neorealist point of view is represented best by the contributions of Kenneth Waltz.

Despite this division, we should note that all the authors that will be stud-ied in this realist section share some basic realist assumptions. At this level, it will suffice to point out that the authors under consideration share a basic pessimistic view of human nature. This view is especially shared by classical realists such as Hobbes, Machiavelli and Thucydides. They also view the state as the primary actor on the international stage. This view is especially shared by postwar realists in the mold of Carr and Morgenthau. They agree that states, like individuals, are power seeking, selfish and antagonistic. Equally important, they view states as rational actors whose actions obey the logic of national security and survival. They also are in agreement, as a consequence of the antagonistic nature of states, that the international system is anarchic, that is it has no central authority with a low potential for progress. This view is an essential neorealist view and is shared by scholars such as Kenneth Waltz, Joseph Grieco, John Mearsheimer and Stephen Walt.

For the realist, this anarchic structure often leads to conflict and, ultimately, war (Waltz 1979). In sum, unlike the idealists, realists are skeptical about the possibility for progress in international politics comparable to that in domes-tic politics. This view of realism is perhaps summed best by Robert Keohane (1986, 7) who argues that realism contains three key assumptions. The first is that realists take the states (or city-states) as units of analysis. The second assumption is that states seek power either as an end in itself or as a means to other ends. The final assumption is that, overall, states behave in rational ways.

a. Classical Realism

As a philosophical tradition, the importance and influence of classical realism on the discipline of international politics can never be stressed enough. This preponderance of political realist thought on the discipline can be measured in terms of its overall impact not only on neorealism and the neoclassical realism of the post–World War period, but it can also be assessed through its impact on the discipline of international relations at large. At the heart of classical realism lies the central idea that human nature is inherently flawed, self-interested and conflict-prone. Having lived through the tragedies of their times, classical realists have seen human nature at its worst. Their painting of man is there-fore a reflection of the worst in man. In this subsection we will analyze the philosophical underpinnings of classical realism through the contributions of the three major thinkers of early realism, notably Thucydides, Machiavelli and Hobbes.

Although widely regarded as a historian, Thucydides is certainly one of the very first writers to have developed a theoretical scheme designed to explain the behavior of states. His analysis of the phenomenon of integration could be framed in terms of a *rapport de force*, which allows more powerful states to conquer weaker states. His historical analysis of the Peloponnesian War (431 BC–404 BC) established the foundations of a theory of the state of nature of international relations. Contrary to the works of previous historians like Herodotus, which attempted to reproduce the historical facts of the same conflict, Thucydides' analysis constitutes one of the earliest attempts to explain the underlying dynamics of international integration through this ancient Greek military conflict. In the process, he reached a level of intellectual, objective and scientific standards not known before him (Bury and Meiggs 1975, 252).

In the Peloponnesian case, the conflict between the Peloponnesian League (led by Sparta) and the Delian League (led by Athens) symbolizes the nature of international relations as an anarchic scene in which the strong do what they can and the weak suffer what they must (Thucydides 1972). For Thucydides, the fundamental cause of the Peloponnesian War was the growth in power of Athens and the concerns that such power caused in Sparta. In his analysis, Thucydides was particularly concerned with one question. Why did Athens and Sparta have to resort to war when they could have lived in peace?

For him, the ultimate meaning of the Peloponnesian War could be found in what it meant for one power and its allies to control the trade routes of Ancient Greece. Since the peace of 445 BC, Pericles had consolidated Athenian resources, made Athens' navy the strongest in the region and concluded in 433 BC an alliance with the strong naval power Corcyra, Corinth's most bitter enemy. In addition, he renewed alliances with Rhegium and Leontini. By these actions, the very food supply of the Peloponnese from Sicily was endangered because with its increased power, Athens would exert a de facto monopoly on trade. In this sense, the Peloponnesian War was a trade war. This is especially true since Corinth appealed to Sparta to take up arms mainly on this basis. Such a call was backed by Megara, a city-state on the brink of economic collapse mainly because of Pericles' economic boycott, and by Aegina, a reluctant member of the Athenian Empire.

As for Niccolo Machiavelli, his influence among classical realists is remarkable. His major contributions to classical realism are contained mainly in The Prince and are multifaceted. This section will focus mainly on his contributions to the international integration scholarship. The Prince is the first analysis of the international system and international society based on the state of nature (Huntzinger 1987, 27). Like his early classical realist colleagues, Machiavelli takes the individual human being as his unit of analysis. Such a unit of analysis is embodied in the prince (leader of the city-state) and his interactions with other members of the community as well as other principalities. In his study, he argues that in order to preserve his power, the prince must essentially be preoccupied with two things. First, he must control the domestic politics within his principality. Second, he must be preoccupied with the objectives of the surrounding principalities (states). This second element of Machiavelli's analysis provides a rare insight into the dynamics of alliance formation.

According to Machiavelli, the behavior of the prince both domestically and internationally is based on fear, intimidation, trickery and constraint. This is the meaning of his famous dictum that the prince must be both a lion and a fox. He must be a lion because, in an anarchic world, weakness is an invitation to be attacked and possibly destroyed. He must be a fox because tricks are necessary under certain circumstances. To be successful, the prince must be cunning and able to perceive threats and deal with them accordingly. The combination of strength and trickery is therefore a necessity for the preservation of the state. According to Machiavelli, a prince must never trust another principality. Since the goal of every principality is to seek power, glory and reputation, the relationship between them is, by definition, a conflicting one. Thus the real profession of every statesman, he argues, is war and the organized used of force. In Machiavelli's view, any statesman who chooses to ignore this law of politics does so at his own risk. "A prince," he contends, "ought to have no other aim or thought, nor select anything else for his study, than war and its rules and discipline" (Machiavelli 1992, 66). For him, too many principalities have been destroyed because their princes chose an alternative to this reality.

The relationship between different principalities is dominated by force and the game that these different actors play in relation to the distribution of power. Thus, the dynamics of international alliance are guided by such logic. Having witnessed two major revolutions, he became convinced of the anarchic and conflicting nature of international relations. He is viewed, to a very large extent, as the founder of the realist school of international relations. He has established a theory that would be developed by other realists, from Thomas Hobbes in the sixteenth century to Hans Morgenthau in the twentieth century.

While there exists indeed a certain continuum in the thought of Thucydides, Machiavelli and Thomas Hobbes, Hobbes provided a more systematic analysis of the international political phenomenon. Michael C. Williams (2005) argues that the claim that international politics is described as an anarchic "Hobbesian state of nature" is a tribute to his contribution to the realist tradition. In fact, Hobbes, in his analysis of politics, systematized an element that has become a central trait of realist thinking: human nature.

With Hobbes, as with Machiavelli, human nature is at the core of the analysis of international relations. The parsimony in his depiction of human nature is informative of his views in more than one regard. Such parsimony reflects both a certain clarity and a troubling pessimism in his view of human nature. Like Machiavelli, Hobbes' personal experience is a key determinant of his thinking. First shaken by his experiences with the English civil war and then by the English revolution, he became convinced of the negative nature of the human condition. Consequently, he views human life in the state of nature as "solitary, poore [sic], nasty, brutish, and short" (Hobbes, 1991, 89). For him, the state of nature is characterized by a perpetual war of everyone against everyone because human beings are constantly driven by the desire to dominate and subjugate other human beings.

The only escape is for everyone to surrender their individual sovereignty to the state, which will in turn guarantee the security of its citizens and maintain order. He uses the metaphor of the Leviathan, a symbol of ultimate power and strength, to refer to the state. Because its citizens have agreed to relinquish their sovereignties to its authority, the state becomes the absolute arbiter among men. He argues that, unfortunately, at the international level, there is no Leviathan that different states could trust their sovereignties and security with. And this, according to Hobbes, explains the anarchic nature of international politics. And since there is no possibility for a Leviathan at the international level, there is no escape and no possibility for progress.

b. Post–World War Realism

In the aftermath of the Second World War, realism became by far the dominant philosophical tradition in international relations. The roots for such an overwhelming presence of realist thinking in the discipline are complex. According to Steve Smith (1987, 203), this fact might be explained by the fact that "[re]alism performs an essentially ideological role in the US." And since the vast majority of international relations theorists, particularly those of the realist persuasion, reside in the US, their influence on the discipline is remarkably strong. International relations, the need for an understanding of the international phenomenon, was born in pain through the unprecedented human and material devastations of two world wars within the time span of twenty-five years.

The main objective of scholars after this unprecedented level of destruction was to understand the causal mechanisms at play in order to avert another catastrophe. So scholars, especially in the United States where the first chairs of international relations were created, set out to understand the causes of this brutal reality called war. Thus, because of the very conditions of its birth amidst the chaos of World War II, international relations thought was strongly tilted toward the study of the causes of war and peace. Realist thinking, as we previously argued, could, however, be traced as far back as the works of Thucydides, Thomas Hobbes and Niccolo Machiavelli. As for post–World War I and post–World War II realism, it emerged out of a growing dissatisfaction with the prevailing views of the time. In fact, this particular strand of political realism started with the rejection of political idealism and utopianism which, in the view of its main proponents, was responsible, to a large extent, for both world wars. Its main proponents are E. H. Carr and Hans Morgenthau.

Although the influence of Marxism on E. H. Carr is quite significant, his contributions to the realist tradition do grant him a place in the realist section of this chapter. He agrees with Marx that individual human beings in isolation are not the determinant factors in the conduct of international relations. He disagrees, however, with Marx in terms of his perception of the key actors on the world stage. Thus, whereas Marx and the Marxists perceive the social class as the unit of analysis, Carr relies on the "national unit" (Carr 1939, 227) and contends that Marx was wrong for exclusively relying on social classes; social classes, according to Carr, lack the cohesive and comprehensive qualities of national units. For this reason, social classes are not nearly as determinant as nation-states in shaping outcomes at the international level. Carr's major criticism, however, was not directed to the Marxists but to liberal idealists whose political philosophy he considered dangerous for the future of the very peace they sought to establish and preserve.

The *Twenty Years' Crisis, 1919–1939* established E. H. Carr as one of the foremost critics of liberal idealism. For him, the liberal idealists are fundamentally wrong in their belief that international relations can be based on a harmony of interest. He contends that international politics is one of profound and irreconcilable conflict of interest. In his view, the ignorance of this basic realist assumption, along with its implications (notably the appeasement policies of the international community), made the Second World War inevitable. In addition, his book can be perceived as a warning that history may repeat itself as a result of a blind idealism. Idealism, in Carr's analysis, is usually compounded with the concept of utopianism, which reflects an analysis of the international system based on wishful thinking. For Carr, this mode of thinking does more harm than good to the functioning of the international system. His argument is based on the rationale that any system of thinking, in order to be meaningful, must be grounded in reality—that is, it must deal with the world as it is and not as we wish it to be. Thus, for him, "the utopia of 1919 was hollow and without substance. It was without influence on the future because it no longer had any roots in the present" (Carr 1939, 224).

Political realism, under its current form, however, was brought to the United States by German intellectual Hans Morgenthau who fled Nazi Germany in the 1930s. His major contribution to realist thought is reflected in his classic international relations textbook entitled *Politics Among Nations: The Struggle for Power and Peace*. Like Carr, he views international politics as an arena of conflict, not one of cooperation and progress. "International politics", he argues, "like all politics, is a struggle for power" (Morgenthau 1973, 27). His views are profoundly influenced by his own experience.

Like the classical philosophers of political realism in the mold of Thomas Hobbes and Niccolo Machiavelli, Morgenthau saw human nature at its worst. His philosophical outlook on the rapport between men as well as that between states was influenced by such an experience. Having lived in Nazi Germany, he experienced human nature at its worst and remained convinced—like Thucydides, Machiavelli and Hobbes—that human nature is essentially bad. For him, there exists in man an insatiable lust for power. Because of this lust for power, or what he calls "animus dominandi," men endlessly seek to dominate others. For him, politics among men, just like politics among states, is characterized by conflict. His perception of this conflicting rapport among men and among states stems from his conviction that one state's gain is another state's loss.

Politics, in his view, is a zero-sum game in which different states compete for power, which he perceives as the ultimate goal of politics (Morgenthau 1946). In the pursuit of this power, he argues, states should not be preoccupied with moral considerations. Rather, their only *modus vivendi* should be the maximization of power. This is the essence of Morgenthau's views on politics, which is power politics. The concept of power politics is indeed at the core of Morgenthau's realist conception of international politics. For Morgenthau, whatever the ultimate goal of international politics may be, power is and will always remain its immediate aim. Thus for him, the basis for international politics is the national interest defined in terms of power. In this sense, a state's foreign policy should be performed with the purposes of advancing its own national interests (Morgenthau 1951). This conception is, to a large extent, shared by all realist and neorealist thinkers.

Like Carr, Morgenthau recognizes that peace is possible under certain circumstances. But unlike liberal idealists such as Woodrow Wilson, he does not believe that peace is achieved through cooperation and appeasement. For him, the balance of power could produce peace (Morgenthau 1973, 200). However, he maintains that for the balance of power to be realized, the existence of a "holder of the balance" is necessary. He sees the role of the latter consisting mainly in maintaining a balance in the rapport between different nations or a coalition of nations. Thus, whenever the balance is about to tilt on one side, because one nation or coalition of nations is becoming too powerful to threaten the balance, the "balancer-nation" must throw himself into the weaker scale. For this reason, he contends that, in international politics, nations have no permanent friends or permanent enemies; they only have permanent interests. Those interests, in his view, should be understood in terms of maintaining the balance of power (Morgenthau 1973, 194). This balance must be maintained by force if necessary. In other words, efforts to stop aggressive states simply by resorting to dialog are naïve and could ultimately lead to war.

c. Neorealism

Neorealist thinking is deeply rooted in the philosophy of Kenneth Waltz. Waltz's philosophical foundation is built from the realist conception of the state as the central unit of analysis. Like the realists, he contends that the number one concern of states is security and survival. He also shares the central realist concepts of power politics and self-help. For him, "the national system is not one of self-help" in the sense that it is governed by a central authority charged with the responsibility to maintain and restore order, but the international system is characterized by an anarchic self-help because there is no central authority (Waltz 1986a, 100). However, unlike the classical realists (e.g., Hobbes) and the neoclassical realists of the post–World War II era (e.g., Morgenthau), Waltz does not focus on human nature as the most important actor in his analysis of the international system. Rather, his neorealist systems theory focuses on the structure of the international system at the expense of other actors.

His rationale for such an option lies in his conviction that the driving force in international politics is the structure of the international system and the results of the effects that derive from such a structure. He views individual political leaders as mere cogs in the wheels of the international structural system. Thus the question of war and peace, in his mind, are determined by the structure of the international system not by individual leaders. The nature of this structure is in turn determined by great powers (Waltz 1979). In this respect, he prefers a bipolar system to a multipolar one. Peace and stability, he argues, are better guaranteed in a two-state system because the preservation of the system, in this case, means the preservation of both powers. In addition, for Waltz, states could be managed better in a bipolar world of states. Waltz's rationale is that with both powers possessing nuclear weapons, the cost of war largely outweighs its benefits. The Cold War "peace," in his view, could be accounted for by the fact that both the United States and the Soviet Union had an equal stake in the preservation of peace and in their realization that a war between them could only bring about mutual destruction. Such is the essence of his argument that "both bipolarity and nuclear weapons promote peace" (Waltz 1986b, 343).

It is also important to note that there are similarities between neorealism and the postwar realism of Morgenthau. As a matter of fact, Waltz shares in Morgenthau's concept of power politics. But there are also some significant differences between Waltz and Morgenthau. Morgenthau, for instance, perceives power politics mainly within the larger context of international politics as a conflicting arena between different states and different temporary alliances of states. Waltz's analysis, on the other hand, is focused on the Cold War era along with the political structure which is derived from it. In other words, for Waltz, the rapport between the two superpowers of the cold war constitutes the prime illustration of power politics at work. This can be explained by the fact that, in Waltz's view, only great powers are capable of affecting in fundamental ways the shape of the international system. Like his realist predecessors, he recognizes the role of states as key actors on the international arena, but he departs from them in the significance he attributes to different states. In this sense, one of Waltz's greatest merits lies in his attempt to pick up from where his realist predecessors like Morgenthau left off. According to Keohane (1986, 15), "the significance of Waltz's theory ... lies less in his initiation of a new line of theoretical inquiry or speculation than in his attempt to systematize political realism into a rigorous, deductive systemic theory of international politics."

III. The Liberal Paradigm

Rooted in the philosophical traditions of John Locke, Jean Jacques Rousseau and Immanuel Kant, the liberal paradigm offers one of the most elaborate theories of international integration. Unlike the realist thinkers of their time, they view individual human beings in an inherently positive light. The relationship between states, which are natural ramifications of individuals, is accordingly viewed by liberals with the same positive light, one in which all states gain. Their philosophy is optimistic in nature and stands in sharp opposition to the pessimistic philosophy of the realist thinkers like Thucydides, Machiavelli and Hobbes. The liberal view was articulated in the seventeenth century by the British liberal philosopher John Locke who made the argument that there exists a significant potential for human progress in modern civil societies and capitalist economies. For him, individual liberty was vital for human progress. Thus the state, in his view, must guarantee freedom to all citizens in order to unleash in each individual the potential for growth and development. For him, the birth of the modern society is inextricably linked to this liberation process.

The French philosopher Jean Jacques Rousseau constitutes another important reference in the tradition of liberal political philosophy. His views are interesting in the sense that, taking human nature as his unit of analysis, Rousseau contends that the state of nature is essentially marked by an absence of conflict. This absence of conflict, in his view, is due to the inherent and basic peaceful nature of man in the state of nature. Ironically, however, Rousseau is not as optimistic when it comes to the rapport between states. His influence on the liberal belief system, however, can be measured in terms of his influence on the foremost champion of liberalism: Immanuel Kant.

The German philosopher Kant is arguably the most influential thinker among the liberal philosophers, especially with respect to the liberal position about international integration. Initially inspired by Rousseau, he departs from his less optimistic views regarding the nature of the relationship between states. He profoundly believed in the possibility for moral progress in man. While he sees and recognizes occasional antagonisms, he nevertheless stresses the possibility for humanity to surmount these antagonisms through a col- lective recognition of a universal law, which would be incorporated into a universal civil society. His argument is based on the fact that he largely sees history as moving in a progressive direction toward a more harmonious and more liberated society (Kant 1992). Thus for him, the moral imperative of life, along with the ever-growing consciousness that men everywhere have regard- ing this imperative, is the engine that drives human societies. The ultimate end of such a drive is a perpetual peace among all free societies. In the analysis which will follow, we will examine the impact of Kant's philosophy on the modern proponents of the liberal peace theory. Like realism, there are many trends of liberalism, including sociological liberalism, economic liberalism and democratic liberalism.

The ideas of the Austrian economist and politician Joseph Schumpeter, those of Karl Deutsch and James Rosenau constitute the cornerstone of socio- logical liberalism. According to Schumpeter (1965), international relations are not the reserved domain of state relations; they also involve a transnational web of relationships. In this respect, sociological liberalism is a questioning of the realist assumption that international relations are the domain of sovereign- state actors. International relations, in their view, are also the direct relations between different people, groups of people, associations and movements that are not confined to any one particular state. In their view—and this position is deeply rooted in the tradition of liberalism in general—the relations between people are usually more peaceful than that between states.

Karl Deutsch and his collaborators (1957, 5), who are arguably the most influential theorists in this tradition, contend that the concept of integration in international relations could be understood in terms of the existence of social groups with a process of political communication, some machinery for enforce- ment and some popular habits of compliance. Deutsch's conceptualization of integration, as we argued previously, is based on his understanding of security communities. This systematic analysis of security communities constitutes Deutsch's major contribution to the integration scholarship. In his study of the transnational phenomenon, Karl Deutsch contends that the greater the degree of transactions between societies, the greater the chances for peace. His argument is based on the notion that the establishment of constant lines of communications and interactions between these societies results in greater integration, which in turn makes them less likely to resort to violence to settle their conflicts (Deutsch et al. 1957). Thus, next to the vertical dimension of international relations, which is made of the relations between states and governments, there exists also a horizontal dimension of international relations, which puts people, movements, intellectuals and social classes directly in contact irrespective of their national origins (Huntzinger 1977). For the majority of sociological liberals, this new trend of cross-state relations constitutes a serious alternative to the state-centered position of the realist paradigm.

Last but not least, James Rosenau is without a doubt one of the most important proponents of sociological liberalism. Rosenau's main interest is on transnational relations at the macro level. He points to the current level of education of individuals in general and to the significance of technological advances to make the argument that transnational activities constitute a central fact of international relations. He sees this cross-state relationship as having a right of its own since, in this environment, the state is increasingly becoming incapable of exercising the capacity for control that it used to enjoy. For this reason, he concludes that even though the state system remains relevant, a new world order may be emerging; an order in which the concept of sovereignty may no longer mean what is used to (Rosenau 1992, 282).

As for democratic liberalism (also known as Republican Liberalism), it is structured around the belief system of the German philosopher Immanuel Kant. Kant's concept of "liberal peace" denotes the idea that liberal democracies are more peaceful and respectful of international law than other systems of governments. In his "Perpetual Peace" argument (1992), Kant contends that world peace could be guaranteed by an alliance of democratic republican states. Revisiting this argument, Michael Doyle points to the "great promise" of democratization across nations (Doyle 1997, 299). The democratic peace argument is based on three major factors.

The first one is related to the fact that democracies are usually built around a political culture of dialog. In democracies, conflicts are resolved by negotiation. Second, a democracy is a system of government by the people. For this reason, going to war is not easy since political leaders must first seek the consent of the people through their elected representatives. This process makes wars very unlikely for one essential reason. Since people are an integral part of the process and since they are inherently peaceful, according the liberal approach, any process based on their consent is rooted in peace. Third, the liberal peace study has a strong economic component. It is based on a system of economic laissez-faire and interdependence, which takes away the centrality of the state as the most important actor in the process. Such an economic interdependence makes wars very costly and therefore functions as an effective deterrent in because the outcome of war could only be measured in terms of losses.

Within democratic liberalism, politics is perceived as a non–zero-sum game. Through cooperation, all parties can gain, albeit unequally, and none lose (Russett 1993, 24). The implication of such a belief system is that world peace could stem from a systematic spread of democracies around the world. On this account there is a marked difference of opinions among the scholars about democratization as a means for world peace. Such differences separate two distinct camps: the proponents of democratization as a recipe for world peace and the institutional liberals.

The first camp, composed of the proponents of democratization, argues that the spread of liberal democracies is a peace factor. In "How Liberalism Produces Democratic Peace," John Owen attempts to "defend the democratic peace proposition" (Owen 1994, 88). For him, the liberal belief system in the tradition of Locke, Rousseau and Kant, one that perceives the same positive and tolerant characteristics of individuals everywhere, is fundamentally a recipe for peace. The basis of his argument is that democracies, because of their inherent institutional arrangements in which the citizens exercise a degree of control over the government, are constrained to seek peace. In addition, these same characteristics make democracies more amenable to form communities for the defense of the democratic ideal.

Owen's contentions are supported by Michael Doyle (1997) and Bruce Russet (1993) who point to the fact that democracies are peaceful toward other democracies. However, the liberal peace theory also has its detractors. In "The Insignificance of the Liberal Peace," David Spiro (1994) defends the proposition that because of the rarity of the chances for war between democratic states, democratic peace could be attributed to pure contingence and chance. His remark is based on Mearsheimer's peace-by-default argument. He observes that owing to the scarcity of democracies in the past, there just were not many chances for them to fight each other, explaining thus the so-called peace among democracies. In this sense, the theory of liberal peace is statistically insignificant and does very little to explain war and peace in international politics.

The second camp is made of institutional liberals. Democratic liberals also share a strong belief in institutions. In their view, an institution can be understood as an international organization such as the United Nations (UN) or the North Atlantic Treaty Organization (NATO). It can also be a set of rules that govern the action of states in given areas such as the military or the economy. Such sets of rules are also known as regimes. Contrary to the realist belief, democratic or institutional liberals do not believe that an international institution is a mere "scrap of paper" totally impotent in the face of strong states. They contend that these institutions serve a purpose and do indeed have an impact on the actions of states. In this sense, they argue that institutions are agents of peace among states (Keohane 1989, Doyle 1997). This argument is based on the constraint that institutions, through the framework of the international legal order, can exercise on state behavior.

Finally, economic liberalism constitutes today one of the dominant theories of economic philosophy in the international economic system. Its influence can be measured in the form of the dominance of classical and neoclassical economics in the world economic system today. This dominance goes hand in hand with the triumph of the Western Bloc and the collapse of the Soviet system in the aftermath of the historic and symbolic fall of the Berlin Wall. In the eyes of the economic liberals, economics is not subordinated to politics. Economic liberals stand in sharp opposition with theories that perceive the economy as a sphere dependent on politics. The original thinker of economic liberalism is eighteenth century British economist Adam Smith. At the heart of Adam Smith's argument there is a belief in the existence of rational actors, of the possibility for economic progress and in the non–zero-sum nature of free trade.

The belief in an "economic laissez-faire" is in fact central to the philosophy of economic liberalism. This argument is based on their contention that markets tend to regulate themselves and do so always in the direction of progress in the absence of political interference. In their view, trade in itself acts like an engine of growth. But in order to be so, it must be unfettered. Their rationale is that regional specialization leads countries to focus on what they do best and thus can not only boost their comparative advantage but they can also increase their income levels in the process (Spero and Hart 1997, 152). Under this logic, they argue, international relations are a non–zero-sum game. Through cooperation, there can only be winners.

In the views of Joan Spero and Jeffrey Hart, the solution to the development needs of the Third World lies in the private financial flows from the developed world that would result from free trade. In other words, the economic liberals advocate a "less state" strategy for the lesser-developed world if they are to dig themselves out of the hole of economic stagnation. Thus, in lieu of the state as a central focus, their attention is driven toward private actors such as private firms and private individuals. They advocate the autonomy of economics over politics. Robert Gilpin (1987, 67), for instance, argues that the unleashing of market forces tends to yield positive results. Thus, for him, the emergence of the modern world itself is the direct result of factors internal to the market.

IV. The Constructivist Paradigm

The origins of the constructivist tradition could be traced back to the thoughts of the Italian philosopher Giambattista Vico. For Vico, the natural environment is a creation of God, but the historical setting is man's creation. In other words, men make all history and all historical constructs, including the state system and the international system. In this, they converge with the critical theorists and postmodernists. Both traditions view the international system is a social construct.

As an emerging paradigm, constructivism is a part of the larger social theories of international politics. This tradition runs directly counter to the realist's assumption that states' preferences are fixed and timeless. In other words, they dispute the realist contention that the maximization of power is the ultimate and immediate aim of states and that states seek power either as an end or as a means toward other ends. Thus, whereas realists analyze state interest as a given, constructivists analyze international politics in the context of the broader social relations that define such a relationship (Hopf 2002; Legro 2005; Wendt 1992).

The constructivist paradigm also runs counter to the realist assumption, the one most clearly articulated by Hans Morgenthau. Morgenthau (1948, 4) explains: "politics, like society in general, is governed by objective laws … the operation of these laws being impervious to our preferences, men will challenge them only at the risk of failure." For the constructivists, state behavior in one direction or another is not predetermined by scientific laws. To the contrary, state behavior is determined by their identities which are neither given nor constant but changing. Cynthia Weber's (2001, 60) claim that state identities and interests are not stable and that they have no pre-given nature could be understood in such light. The concept of identity can be understood as a set of common characteristics which is shared by a group of states and which sets them apart from other states or other groups of states.

Like realism and liberalism, there are many constructivist strands. The first strand is rooted in the belief that states' interests and identities are intertwined and that those identities are shaped by interactions with other states (Adler and Barnett 1998; Hall and Jones 1999). On this account, constructivists argue that the analysis of structural realism omits what they consider to be a determinant factor, notably the intersubjectively shared ideas that shape behavior by constituting the identities and interests of actors. Such identities, according to Alexander Wendt (1992), determine what the nature of the relationship between different states might be irrespective of structure. His often-cited phrase, "Anarchy is what States make of it." should be understood in this light. In other words, Wendt accepts the realist idea that the international system is anarchic but disagrees with the realists that such anarchy leads to international conflict. Wendt argues that the existence of anarchy is not a sufficient condition for war. Rather, it is the perception that different states have about such anarchic situations that determines whether war could occur or not. The examples of Germany and France, which have been bitter enemies in the two major wars of the twentieth century and between whom the prospects of a war seem preposterous today, could be a prime example.

According to the constructivists, this peace between Germany and France is the product of the new ways in which the two states and their elites perceive themselves and each other as a result of a process. Thus, in Wendt's views, as in those of Peter Katzenstein (1996), Friedrich Kratochwil (1989) and Nicholas Onuf (1989), the concept of process holds a central place. This runs counter to Waltz's and the positivist argument of the neorealists. In fact, Wendt's argument, to a large extent, constitutes a critical assessment of the neorealist assumptions. Whereas neorealists in the mold of Waltz argue in favor of the primacy of structure over process, he is convinced to the contrary. In other words, he maintains that the anarchic and self-help nature of international politics is a product of process not structure. This leads him to view Waltz's concept of balance of power as a "balance of threats" (Wendt 1992, 397).

Wendt's argument is based on the centrality of the notion of perception of the significance of power over its distribution. "US military power," he argues, "has a different significance for Canada than for Cuba, despite their similar 'structural' positions, just as British missiles have a different significance for the United States than do Soviet missiles" (Wendt 1992, 398). In this respect, the critical element as far as the relationship between these states is determined less by the structure of the system than by the perceptions of these different states. For the constructivists, shared history, shared alliances and shared norms tell the United States that the UK is not a threat even though its military may be more powerful than that of other states, including North Korea and Iran (states that are not bound to the United States by a shared identity).

Thus, the constructivists contend that the relationship between two different states is determined less by the military capabilities and interests of the potential adversaries and more by their identities. As Wendt (1999) explains, these state identities are complex and changing, and they arise from interactions with other states—often through a process of socialization. Equally important, he argues that, over time, states can conceptualize one another in ways that make the security dilemma, arms races or the other effects of anarchy obsolete. Europe, a continent at the center of two of the deadliest military conflicts in the first half of the twentieth century and where a major armed conflict has become unthinkable, is, according to the constructivists, the prime illustration of the potency of the transformational power of identity. Jeffrey Checkel (2000) attributes these transformations to institutions, regimes, norms and changes in identity not power politics.

As for the second strand of constructivism, it is rooted in a belief about the capacity of international norms to constrain state action. Unlike the realists and neoliberals who contend that states make decisions based on a logic of consequences, constructivist thought is geared toward a logic of appropriateness. In other words, whereas the realists contend that states ask what will happen to them if they behave a certain way, the constructivists argue that states ask how they should behave in a given situation (March and Olsen 1998).

These norms spread around the world through three major vehicles. The first vehicle is made of individuals, also known as norm entrepreneurs, who through their travels, writings and meetings with elites in a variety of countries help change ideas, views and perceptions and encourage certain norms. The second vehicle is made of social movements and nongovernmental organizations. The anti-Apartheid movement, for instance, is one of the most prominent of these social movements. It played a key role in encouraging the development of a global norm of racial equality. The third vehicle is made of international organizations such as the United Nations, the European Union and the African Union, which can diffuse norms of what is appropriate and inappropriate behavior at the international level.

In sum, this variety of constructivism, which focuses on the power of international norms, argues that new ideas and norms, rather than power and self-interest, could drive state behavior (Keck and Sikkink 1998). Jeffrey Checkel (2001) illustrates this notion quite well by pointing to the role of the European Union in socializing elites in new member states. These elites, despite being from a former rival bloc with a different set of identities, are integrated into a new system through a socialization process.

Thus, following the same logic, this strand of the constructivist tradition has also to be understood in terms of the emerging norms in international human rights. Daniel C. Thomas' analysis of the phenomenon of the "logic of appropriateness" constitutes a remarkable contribution to the debate on norm forming in the arena of international human rights (Thomas 2001, 13). His argument runs counter the realist assumption. He contends that states are, in part, the creation of the international society. For this reason he perceives the motives that drive state action as a reflection of the impact of international norms on state behavior. In this direction, he argues that the Helsinki accords in 1975 played a crucial role in the demise of the Soviet Union precisely because they garnered a level of consciousness in the states of the Eastern Bloc. This consciousness translated into the irruption of social movements in these different states and ultimately caused the fundamental changes that resulted in the collapse of the communist system.

V. Conclusion

In sum, it is important to point out that these three paradigms offer some of the most elaborate explanations on the conditions under which communities in general and security communities in particular emerge at the international level. The explanatory power of these three paradigms in explaining the rise of communities in general and African security communities in particular will be tested in the following chapters, especially in Chapters 4, 5, and 6. However, an overview of Africa's communities may be necessary to set the stage for such a test.

Chapter 3
Africa's Communities

The main goal of this chapter is to introduce both Africa's early and modern communities. While concentrating on the three modern African security communities, the brief description of historical security communities in Africa suggests the links between past and present in the history of African international relations. In the process, this chapter will seek to answer one central question: Why do different states delegate their national sovereignties to regional or international structures? Broadly, the formation of integrated communities in Africa has evolved in two major stages. The first stage can be traced back to the formation of the earliest integrated communities in the form of empires. In this chapter, our attention will be focused on three such major early communities, including the Kanem Empire, the Mali Empire and the Jolof Empire. The second major stage finds its roots in the birth of the first modern African states in the 1960s, corresponding to the first wave of independence within the African continent. This chapter will focus of three such major modern communities, including the African Union (AU), the Economic Community of West African States (ECOWAS), and the Southern African Development Community (SADC). These modern communities constitute natural continuations of Africa's early communities.

I. Africa's Early Communities

The origins of African integration can be traced back to Africa's early communities. According to most historians, the earliest known evidence for the emergence of human society comes from East and Northeast Africa (Fage 1995, 1). Such societies evolved into communities, which integrated smaller entities and kingdoms into supranational entities or empires. Such empires rose in Africa as early as the seventh century CE according to available records. However, it is likely that human communities existed much earlier, but because no written evidence is available, historians have only speculated about their size and significance. As Phillip Curtin (1995) noted, some of the earliest African states, which formed the basis for the African empires, have indeed existed before the earliest Western states.

It is important to note that these communities were formed largely to secure the trading routes, which run across the desert edges and the coastal areas of sub-Saharan Africa. These trade routes constituted life savers for most early African societies. Thus Africa's empires emerged to coordinate the economic activity in a given region and to secure commerce between the different societies that populated given geographical locations. As Phillip Curtin (1995, 73) puts it, early West African states and empires rose in similar contexts as states elsewhere, in the sense that Africa's early empires arose "to meet the needs of trade and defense." Such economic activities revolved around a variety of commodities, including gold, ivory, agricultural products, etc. For all these reasons, Africa's early communities have been referred to as trading empires.

It is equally important to note—without excluding much earlier African empires such as Nubia, Kemet, Axum, etc.—that the formation of Africa's early empires went hand in hand with the spread of Islam. The primary reason is that Islam was the religion of their most important trading partners from the north. In addition, the attractiveness of Islam for the trading empires of Africa could also be measured in terms of the invaluable skill of literacy, which the Arab merchants brought with them. Thus, while many of Africa's early rulers accepted Islam with a deep conviction, others accepted Islam for practical purposes. Most prominent among these rulers were the Mais (emperors) of Kanem and the Mansas (emperors) of Mali, especially Mansa Musa. Even those rulers who rejected Islam outright for themselves, like the rulers of the Ghana Empire, still welcomed Muslim merchants. For all these reasons, the first written references of the political, economic and cultural organization of Africa's early empires are provided by Muslim scholars (Fage 1995, 55). These early communities included Kanem (700 AD–1376 AD), Ghana (750 AD–1076 AD), Bachwezi (1200 AD–1300 AD), Mali (1235 AD–1645 AD), Jolof (1350 AD–1890 AD) and Songhai (1375 AD–1591 AD). In this section, we will briefly discuss the cases of Kanem, Mali and Jolof.

a. The Kanem Empire

As one of the oldest political powers in Africa (Cohen 1967, 12), the empire of Kanem reached the peak of its existence approximately between the eighth and

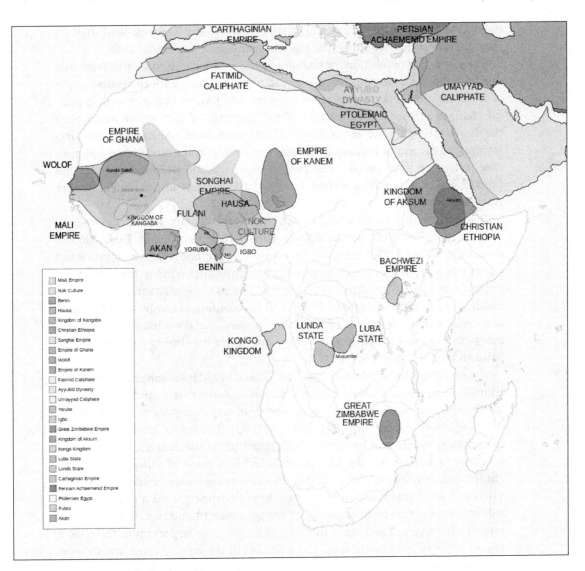

Figure 1: The Kanem Empire

the fourteenth century and encompassed territories that are part of the modern day states of Chad, Libya, Sudan as well as significant portions of Nigeria, Cameroon and Niger. In addition, the empire of Kanem was made of people from different ethnic and linguistic backgrounds, which included a variety of African people, Arabs and Berbers. The formation of Kanem is the result of the migration of nomadic peoples called the Zaghawa who originated from the northeast and were forced to travel into the more fertile areas bordering Lake Chad. At their arrival, the Zaghawa met a non-nomadic people, the So, who had already engineered a sophisticated though noncentralized society of city-states protected by walls. After adopting many of the customs of the So and fighting many wars with them, the Zaghawa eventually dominated the So (Stride and

Ifeka 1971, 115). In the aftermath of their victory, the Zaghawa instituted an administration that would be the envy of many societies of that time.

However, the revolutionary changes in the political, cultural and economic organization of the Kanem Empire would not take place until the introduction of Islam in 1085. The introduction of Islam into Kanem brought with it radical changes as Arabic became the official language of the empire along with the Islamization of the entire imperial administration. Although Islam also introduced the era of literacy in an oral environment, it encountered a significant resistance from people who favored their traditional belief systems and practices. By the twelfth century, however, Islamic rule in the Kanem Empire was quasi total.

The empire of Kanem would become stronger economically and politically after merging with the Bornu Empire during the reign of Mai Idris Alooma from 1575 to 1610. This merging gave an economic boost to the empire since Bornu was a much greener land, which was significant owing to the utmost importance of agriculture during this period. The most significant political, economic and military reorganization of Bornu was undertaken by Ali Ghajedeni who built a new capital called Birni Ngazargamu, "the walled fortress." Such reorganization was undertaken with the goal of reestablishing control over the Saharan trade (Cohen 1967, 15).

Thus, when Idris Alooma came to power with both empires under his control, he proceeded to organize the empire in ways that would make it more manageable. Thus, the empire comprised four major centers of power, which were organized hierarchically (Cohen 1967, 92). The lower level was made of households, wards and hamlets, which constituted the foundational political units of the Kanuri society. The second level was made of villages, which included different households, wards and hamlets and were headed by lawans. The third level was made of districts. These districts played a crucial role in collecting taxes for the functioning of the government and sustaining the military of the empire. The Kanuri military was especially important in the overall organization of the empire since the revenues of the empire came mainly from tribute or booty from conquered territories and from duties that emanated from the trans-Saharan trade. Such trade revolved around products as diverse as cotton, kola nuts, ivory, ostrich feathers, perfume, wax, hides, salt, horses, silks, glass, muskets and copper. Finally, at the top level, there was the central government headed by the Shehu who appoints and installs all district heads after consulting his councils and local representatives.

The soundness of the reorganization of Kanem-Bornu is credited to Idris Alooma who is often remembered for his military, administrative and diplomatic skills. His reforms, for instance, included the introduction of fixed military camps, permanent sieges, armored horses and riders as well as the use of Berber camelry, Kotoko boatmen, and iron-helmeted musketeers trained by Turkish military advisers. In addition, Alooma's diplomatic corps comprised over 200 diplomatic representations. As far as his administrative reforms are concerned, Alooma initiated a number of legal and administrative reforms based mainly on the Sharia (Islamic law).

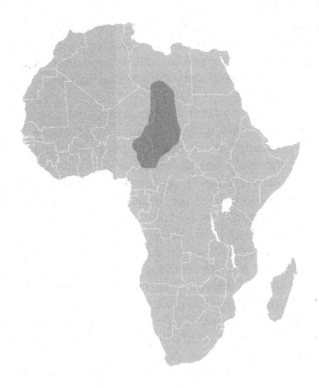

Figure 2. The Mali Empire

b. The Mali Empire

Also known as the Manding Empire, the Mali Empire was founded by Sundiata Keita and became world renowned for its impressive administrative organization. Such organization was backed by a constitution that could be envied by many modern day constitutions. Such a constitution could also rival any ancient legal document, including the Magna Carta published in 1215. Known as the Kouroukan Fouga or Kurukan Fuga, this Manden constitution or charter established the system of government of the Mali Empire (1235–1546) based on a coherent system of laws which all people within the empire were expected to live by (Cisse 2003). The transmission of the content of this historical legal document was the responsibility of a generation of djelis or griots. Thus, much of the history of the Mali Empire, including its system of government, have been preserved and transmitted to the next generations thanks to the griots who played the functions of modern day historians.

At its height, from approximately 1235 AD to 1600 AD, the Mali Empire engulfed an area larger than Western Europe and consisted of numerous kingdoms and provinces. Originally created as a federation of the Mandinka tribes known as Manden Kurufa (literally Manden federation), the Mali Empire eventually took under its umbrella millions of people from nearly every ethnic group living in West Africa. The original Manden federation, founded by Mari

Djata I, was made of the "three freely allied states" of Mali—namely, Mema, Wagadou and the so-called Twelve Doors of Mali. The Twelve Doors of Mali were a coalition of conquered or allied territories, mostly within Manden, who swore allegiance to the emperor of Mali. In return for their allegiance, their leaders were made "farbas," a title for a representative of the emperor in their respective old kingdoms.

The empire of Mali was built as a remarkable political, economic and military organization. The political organization of the Mali Empire was a model of political federation. Political historian Joseph Ki-Zerbo (1978) explains: as the federal capital, Niani was the center of authority of the empire and was governed by a Mansa (emperor). However, the farther a person traveled from Niani, the more decentralized the emperor's power became. This decentralized system, however, did not constitute an impediment for territorial control and for the collection of taxes. The empire was divided into provinces each governed by a Dya-Mana-Tigi, the equivalent of a governor chosen mostly through election and inheritance and approved by the emperor. Each province was composed of districts made of villages. Each district was administered by a Kafo-Tigi, the equivalent of a county-master. At the bottom of the scale, but more important in some respects, were the village units administered by Dugu-Tigis who were also the head of village cults. These local governments were charged with the handsome responsibility of guaranteeing that the empire had the economic means of its politics (Stride and Ifeka 1971, 60).

As for its economic organization, the Mali Empire was built primarily around trade and its regulation. Such trade revolved around three major goods: gold, salt and copper. Consequently, the empire excised taxes on every ounce of gold, salt or copper that entered its borders. However, as Stride and Ifeka explain in reference to Ibn Battuta, who provides the most detailed account of Mali, there was a sense of justice in the process. Stride and Ifeka explain that Ibn Battuta was more than impressed by the quality of the people and their system of government, which was based on the rule of law. Citing the example of the corrupt governor of Walata, one of the provinces of Mali, who was stripped of his possession and privileges, Ibn Battuta claims that the government of the Mali Empire rivaled anything he had seen in North Africa or Asia, where he travelled extensively (Stride and Ifeka 1971, 57).

In addition, because trade was so crucial to the survival of the empire, its founder, Sundiata, personally managed the terms of the trade. As an illustration, he fixed exchange rates for common products. Moreover, the Farbas of the empire, who were picked by the emperor and entrusted with safeguarding imperial interests, played a uniquely important economic function in the system (Cooley 1966, 63). Among the most important duties of the farba were reporting on the activities of the territory, collecting taxes and ensuring that Niani's orders were followed by the local governments. The farba was also empowered with the privilege of removing power from the local administrations and raising an army in local areas for defense or putting down rebellions (Levitzion 1963).

Finally, the importance of the third major component of the organization of Mali Empire—its military—can never be stressed enough. If anything, the empire expanded largely on the basis of military conquests and annexations. The number, the frequency and the rate of success of such conquests in the late thirteenth century and throughout the fourteenth century constitute a prime illustration of the high levels of military organization of the empire. Although Sundiata Keita is credited with at least the initial organization of the Manding war machine, the machine went through radical changes before reaching the legendary proportions proclaimed by historians. In this respect, the empire's military capabilities go hand in hand with its political and economic organization—a steady source of tax revenues and a stable government were essential to sustaining a semiprofessional and full-time army. At its height, the Mali Empire was able to mobilize, on a consistent basis and on short notice, an army of 100,000 men including 10,000 cavalry (Sarr 1991, 92). This is the essential reason the Mali Empire, beginning in the last quarter of the thirteenth century, was able to project its power and influence beyond its original borders.

The organization of the army was also based on a very efficient strategy— the command of the army was divided into two distinct geographical command centers: the northern command center and the southern command center led by members of Mali's warrior elite known as the *ton-ta-jon-ta-ni-woro* (literally the sixteen slave carriers of quiver). Each of these representatives, also known as *ton-tigi* (quiver-master), constitutes a military adviser to the emperor. Finally, because of its economic might, the empire was able to afford a wide range of weapons based the location and the traditions of the local troops.

c. The Jolof Empire

Also known as the Wolof Empire, the Jolof Empire comprised much of the West African modern states of Senegal and the Gambia and extended as far inland as the Mandigo state of Mali (Stride and Ifeka 1971, 22). The earliest written accounts of the Jolof Empire are provided by the Portuguese who

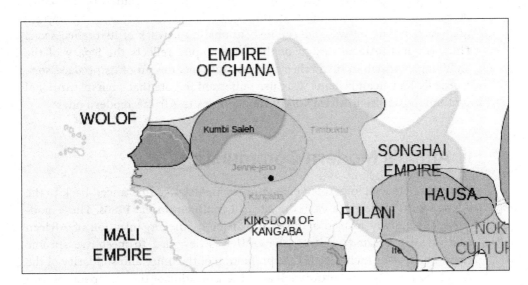

Figure 3: The Wolof, or Jolof, Empire

documented a detailed account of a very advanced political system (Fage and Oliver 1975, 456). The Jolof Empire was a highly hierarchical system composed of different classes of royal and nonroyal nobles, freemen, occupational castes and slaves. Occupational castes included blacksmiths, jewellers, tanners, tailors, musicians and griots (Fage and Oliver 1975, 484). Each of these classes played a determinant role in society. Blacksmiths, for instance, played a crucial role for their ability to make weapons of war. In addition, they enjoyed a reputation of trust for their ability to mediate disputes fairly. As for griots, they played the very important role of chroniclers and advisors, without whom much of the history of early Jolof would be unknown (Stride and Ifeka 1971, 26).

The Jolof Empire reached its peak during the medieval era between approximately 1350 and 1890. Founded by Ndyadyane Ndyaye, the Jolof Empire epitomized Rousseau's concept of voluntary association. The process started with a northern state called Waalo, later joined by Sine, Kayor, Baol and Saloum (all previously independent states). All of these states were tributary to the landlocked state of Djolof.

The administrative center of the Jolof Empire was Linguère, the capital city, from where the Burba Jolof, the head of the Jolof Empire, ruled the federal system. Each state was administered by its own ruler appointed from the descendants of the founder of the state. State rulers were chosen by their respective nobles, while the Burba Jolof was selected by a college of electors which also included the rulers of the five kingdoms (Fage and Oliver 1975, 457). The five states were governed respectively by the Bur of Waalo, the Damel of Kayor, the Teny of Baol as well as the two Lamans of the states of Sine and Saloum. One of the most important administrative features of the organization of the Jolof Empire is the autonomy which was accorded to the five states of the union. They were, however, expected to cooperate with the central authority of the Burba Jolof on matters of defense, trade and the provision of imperial revenue (Stride and Ifeka 1971, 25).

Finally, it is also important to note that there is a continuum in the political, economic and cultural organization of the different early African empires since each empire draws from the institutional framework of its predecessors. Thus, the institutional design of the Jolof Empire reflects the legacy of the Mali Empire which in turn reflects the institutional design of its predecessors, especially Kanem and Ghana. It is also important to note that such institutional continuum goes from Africa's early communities to Africa's modern ones.

II. Africa's Modern Communities

The rise of modern integrated communities in Africa can be traced back to the birth of most modern states in the African continent in the 1960s. These modern states quickly formed a supranational body, the Organization of African Unity (OAU). Created in 1963, the OAU was designed to meet five specific goals. These goals included: (1) the promotion of the unity and solidarity of the African states, (2) the coordination and intensification of their cooperation and efforts to achieve a better life for the peoples of Africa, (3) the defense of the sovereignty and the territorial integrity and independence of African states, (4) the eradication of all forms of colonialism in Africa, and (5) the promotion of international cooperation. The results of the OAU did not measure up to the enthusiasm associated with its birth. Thus, the successor of the OAU, the AU, emerged out of a growing realization that the OAU was becoming inadequate to cope with the challenges that Africa faced in the twenty-first century. As for ECOWAS and the SADC, they emerged primarily out of the realization that different (sub) regions needed institutions of proximity that could guarantee regional stability, which is a sine qua non condition for development. In addition, both (sub) regional communities work closely with the AU and complement its actions. As Oosthuizen (2006, 214) points out, referring specifically to the SADC, Africa's (sub) regional communities constitute parts of the African Union's security architecture.

a. The African Union

Although the structure of the African Union is built in large part from the remains of the Organization of African Unity, which disbanded in 2001, the African Union is largely inspired by the European Union. Thus, the resemblances between the African Union and the Organization of African Unity on one hand and the European Union on the other hand include their structural and institutional designs as well as their organic compositions. In this sense, this section will start with a brief overview of the Organization of African Unity and will move toward a comparative description between the African Union and the European Union.

Established in Addis Ababa, Ethiopia, on May 25, 1963, the Organization of African Unity (OAU) began as a union of thirty-two independent African states and eventually enlisted its fifty-third state when post-Apartheid South Africa joined the organization on May 23, 1994. Established in a time of need for Africa's independence, the OAU was created to free the continent of colonial rule and to promote the unity of the African continent.

The structure of the OAU, which is enunciated in Article VII of the charter of the organization, was made of four major institutions. These institutions include the assembly of heads of state and governments; the council of ministers; the general secretariat and the commission of mediation, conciliation and arbitration (Addona 1969, 122). In addition, the OAU relied on a variety of specialized agencies for its daily operations. Such agencies included the African Accounting Council, the African Bureau for Educational Sciences, the African Civil Aviation Commission, the Pan-African News Agency, the Pan-African Postal Union, the Pan-African Railways Union, the Pan-African Telecommunications Union and the Supreme Council for Sports in Africa. It is important to note that most of these agencies have survived the OAU and have been incorporated into the African Union.

However, despite the ideals inscribed in its constitutive act, the OAU would be marred with internal conflicts that would paralyze the institution and lead to its ultimate implosion. The seeds of the destruction of the OAU are rooted in the conditions in which the organization was born. The OAU was created amidst intense tensions amongst the leaders of the newly freed states of Africa. The Addis Ababa meeting, which gave birth to the OAU, was thus the product of enormous compromises between the Casablanca faction and the Monrovia faction. The first one, the Casablanca group, was composed of Ghana, Guinea, Mali, Egypt, Algeria and Morocco; the second one, the Monrovia group, was essentially made of Nigeria, Liberia, Senegal, Ivory Coast, Cameroon and Togo. More than anything else, the Addis Ababa summit was a shock between different leadership styles with very distinct political visions in terms of what kind of integration scheme Africa needed in its efforts to rid to continent of the insecurity scourge which impeded its economic takeoff.

Thus, while the Monrovia group argued for a limited integration mechanism that would safeguard the total sovereignties of all individual African states, the Casablanca group, under the leadership of Dr. Kwame Nkrumah of Ghana, saw the immediate formation of an amalgamated community as the only way for salvation. As a result, the OAU, born amidst such circumstances, was the product of a compromise, which the organization never managed to transcend. Pulled to the right by the partisans of an amalgamated community and to the left by the partisan of a looser association, the OAU remained marred in internal contradictions and crises.

In fact, Article 3(2) of the OAU Charter is one of the most patent indications of a crisis, which nagged the OAU and especially its conflict management mechanism. By laying a strong emphasis on the acceptance of the borders of the Berlin Conference of 1884–1885[1] and on the principle of nonintervention in the affairs of other states, the OAU constitutes a hindrance to conflict resolution in Africa. In 1981, an attempt was made to correct this problem with the institution of an "inter-African Force." This force was designed to deal with the crisis in Chad in 1981 and beyond, if it proved successful. The OAU, however, failed in this crucial attempt and was never able to transcend the overwhelming obstacle to regional security. Comfort Ero attributes such failure to the following issues:

> inadequate planning, confusion over the mandate, absence of an OAU command and control structure, the perceived partiality of some troop-contributing countries, minimal financial and logistic resources and, above all, the lack of political will, not just of the parties to the conflict, but also of third-party mediators in the surrounding region (Ero 2000, 1).

The tragic case of Rwanda with over 800,000 Tutsis and moderate Hutus killed in the spring of 1994 constitutes a prime illustration of the resounding failure of the continental organization to overcome Africa's security dilemma. While most analysts agree that the direct cause of the genocide was the incitement of the country's Hutu majority against the Tutsi minority by a small group

---

1   The Berlin Conference was called for by Portugal and organized by Otto von Bismarck, the first Chancellor of Germany. The goal of the conference was to divide up Africa amongst the Western powers. The artificial borders of Africa as we know them today are a result of that conference.

among the Rwandan governing class, there is little doubt that the paralysis of the continental organization was a facilitating cause.

In addition, the OAU also failed to be a peace broker and a peace keeper in a variety of other African conflicts. The Ethiopia-Eritrea border disputes and the long-fought conflicts in a wide variety of other African countries (e.g., Sierra Leone, the Democratic Republic of the Congo, the Republic of the Congo, and Sudan) are signs of a continent with an ailing continental organization. Instead of a genuine attempt to address the urgent needs of a continent in crisis, the OAU, in its last days, continued to be a club where dictators and weak democrats met to talk with no clear sense of purpose. In this respect, CNN's European Political Editor Robin Oakley's (2001) reference to the OAU as a talking shop reflected faithfully the general atmosphere around an organization in disarray. The African Union emerged in such context to replace an obsolete Organization of African Unity.

Although the structure of the African Union is built in large part from the remains of the Organization of African Unity, as we argued previously, the African Union is largely inspired by the European Union. First, just like the case of the European Commission for the European Union, the bureaucracy of the African Union rests with the African Commission, which is headquartered in Addis Abba in Ethiopia. Second, like the European Commission, the African Union's Commission is primarily responsible for the administration and coordination of the African Union's activities and meetings. Such similarities also extend to the two Parliaments. Both organizations function with legislative bodies. Headquartered in Midrand (South Africa), the Pan-African Parliament is made up of 265 elected representatives from all fifty-three-member states of the African Union. Like the European Parliament, it works as a watchdog over the African Commission. It is designed to facilitate popular and civil-society participation in the processes of democratic governance among the member states.

One of the final and equally important similarities includes the institution of the Council of Ministers. This Council, which is also modeled after the European Union's Council of Ministers, consists mainly of ministers of member states designated by their respective governments. This Council intervenes and decides on issues as diverse as security, foreign trade, agriculture, communications, etc.; is accountable to the Assembly and prepares material for the Assembly to discuss and approve. Like the European Union, the African Union also comprises specialized commissions, which deal with a wide range of issues including economics, transport, communications and education. Like its European counterpart, the African Union counts on a variety of specialized agencies including the Pan-African News Agency, the Pan-African Postal Union and the Scientific, Technical, and Research Commission.

However, the African Union departs in some fundamental ways from the European Union. The Assembly of the African Union constitutes, in fact, one of the departures from the European Union and is made of the heads of state and government of all member states. It is the policy-making organ of the African Union. It meets annually and plays the role of policy coordinator. It, inter alia, approves decisions made at the periodic meetings of the Council of Ministers. It is designed to involve member states at the highest level. In addition, because of the unique concerns for peace and security throughout much of the African continent, the African Union departs from the European Union in its institution of the Commission of Mediation, Conciliation and Arbitration. This Commission is endowed with the responsibility of handling efforts to resolve disputes between member states.

However, significant these differences or similarities between the European Union and the African Union might be, they pale in comparison with the enormous differences in the historical and institutional evolutions between the two communities. In fact, the African Union emerged out of very different sets of circumstances from the European Union.

The African Union (AU) is an intergovernmental organization consisting of fifty-three African nations. Established on July 8, 2002, the AU was created as a successor to the Organization of African Unity (OAU). Although the idea of the African Union goes back to the independence days of Africa, it was rekindled at the Syrte Summit in September 1999, when Libya's charismatic leader Muammar Khaddafi launched the idea of a United States of Africa in place of a malfunctioning Organization of African Unity. Thus, the new organization was created to perform essential functions that the OAU could not. Such objectives include the need to accelerate the political and socioeconomic integration of the continent, to promote and defend African common positions on issues of interest to the continent and its peoples, to achieve peace and security in Africa and to promote democratic institutions, good governance and human rights.

Broadly, the emergence of the African Union, however, can also be understood as a combination of external and internal factors. The external factors are related to a post–Cold War era, which called for a new way of solving Africa's problems. It is often argued that the fall of the Berlin Wall opened a new era in international politics. The same is true for African politics. The symbolic event of November 9, 1989, in the capital city of Germany, indeed, ushered African politics into a new era. The collapse of the Soviet Bloc and the subsequent retrenchment and withdrawal of superpowers from many parts of the developing world played a crucial role in impelling countries that previously depended on superpower support to rethink their security options (Conteh-Morgan 1998, 1). The emergence of the African Union has to be understood also in light of this particular context of superpower disengagement.

As for the internal factors to the creation of the AU, they are related to the aforementioned external factors in the sense that the end of the strategic competition in Africa among the world's two major power blocs also signified the end of external support for the security of Africa. In this respect, the end of the Cold War meant that Africa's security would, first and foremost, be Africa's business. In this light, the African Union was set up to overcome the security dilemma[2] that threatened the survival and well-being of African states. It was created to complement and reinforce existing regional security communities such as ECOWAS in West Africa and the SADC in southern Africa.

---

2   The concept of security dilemma was coined by John Herz in his 1951 book *entitled Political Realism and Political Idealism*. The concept is used in international relations to describe a situation in which two or more states are drawn into conflict or even war over security concerns.

ECOWAS, for instance, did set up the Economic Community of West African States Monitoring Group (ECOMOG)—a West African multilateral armed force designed to work along similar lines to NATO with Nigeria as its main provider. The SADC followed a similar institutional evolution as ECOWAS in the sense that it started as a primarily economic entity and evolved into a security entity.

b. ECOWAS

The Economic Community of West African States (ECOWAS) is a voluntary regional organization made of fifteen West African states[3]. It was founded on May 28, 1975, at Lagos in Nigeria with the original mission of promoting economic integration as well as addressing social and development challenges. In this respect, the treaty of Lagos, which gave birth to the West African regional organization, stipulated in no uncertain terms that its goal was to achieve "collective self-sufficiency" for its member states through the creation of a single large trading bloc. Today, however, ECOWAS has emerged as a major regional security actor (Mortimer 1996; Nivet 2006, 13). The fundamental reason for this mutation from a primarily economic community to a security community resides in the realization that the flow of goods, which leads to well functioning economies and societies, is not possible without a minimum of regional security. In this respect, the evolutionary pattern of ECOWAS is similar to those of Africa's early communities, which were discussed earlier in this chapter.

ECOWAS' mutation from a primarily economic community to a security community can largely be measured in terms of the institution of the Economic Community of West African States Monitoring Group (ECOMOG), which is a West African multilateral armed force. ECOMOG is a formal arrangement for the separate armies of West Africa to work together along similar lines to the North Atlantic Treaty Organization (NATO). It is structured around Nigerian armed forces and economic resources with the support of the armed forces of ECOWAS member states. ECOMOG is controlled by the authority of the heads of state of ECOWAS. The exercise of such authority rests with the head of state who has been elected by his colleagues as the chairperson of ECOWAS. The chairperson, in turn, usually acts on behalf of all heads of state of the Community. As for the daily management of the organization, it is handled by the ECOWAS Secretariat, which is headed by an executive secretary. Military operations are handled by the force commander.

In addition, there are two major supervisory political structures which decide on strategic matters that are necessary for the security of the Community: the Defense Council and the Defense Commission. The first political structure, the Defense Council, is headed by the chairperson of the Community and is made up of the ministers of Defense and Foreign Affairs of member states. Its primary purpose is to examine the situation on the ground and decide what strategy and means of intervention need to be adopted. The second political

---

3   The fifteen member states of ECOWAS are Benin, Burkina Faso, Cape Verde, Côte D'Ivoire, the Gambia, Ghana, Guinea, Guinea Bissau, Liberia, Mali, Niger, Nigeria, Senegal, Sierra Leone and Togo. Mauritania withdrew from ECOWAS in 2002.

structure, the Defense Commission, is composed of chiefs of defense staff of the armed forces of member states. Its primary purpose is to give technical advice on military operations (Khobe 2000). Most notable among ECOMOG's interventions are the first Liberian civil war in 1990, the Sierra Leonean civil war in 1997, the Guinea Bissauan civil war in 1999, the Guinean-Liberian border crisis in 2001 and the 2003 Liberian second civil war.

However, although the immediate cause of the creation of ECOMOG is directly related to the Liberian conflict, which caused a grave menace to the security of the entire West African region, the idea of transforming ECOWAS into a security community goes back to the 1978 adoption of the Protocol on Non-Aggression by the heads of state and governments of ECOWAS member states. Article 2 of this protocol clearly stipulates that member states shall refrain from "committing, encouraging or condoning the acts of subversion, hostility or aggression against the territorial integrity or political independence of member states." However the impact of this protocol on the stability of the West African Community was at best minimal as it did little to prevent military coups and regime instability throughout the region. So building from the weakness of the 1978 protocol, West African leaders sought to create a new security concept.

Thus, the signing of the Protocol on Mutual Defense Assistance in Freetown, Sierra Leone, on May 29, 1981, by several ECOWAS members could be understood in such light. Most importantly, the provisions of this protocol included the establishment of an Allied Armed Force of the Community (AAFC) designed to deal with threats to the security of persons and goods in the West African community. This protocol went a step further in its language by stipulating in Article 2 that "any armed threat or aggression directed against any Member State shall constitute a threat or aggression against the entire Community." However, this second protocol, in turn, was not particularly effective in dealing with the new kinds of conflicts that erupted throughout the West African region in the late 1980s and early 1990s. Such conflicts were characterized by their internal origins as opposed to the external threats that the preceding protocols dwelt so much on. The Liberian case constitutes one of the primary examples of the evolving nature of these conflicts. The emergence of ECOMOG, which marks the transformation of ECOWAS from a purely economic entity to a security community, has to be placed within this specific context.

c. The SADC

The Southern African Development Community (SADC) emerged in circumstances similar to those of ECOWAS. It was originally created to face the challenges of its member states. Those challenges are wide ranging and go from the social to the economic. They are also related to trade flows and the problems associated with such trade flows in the absence of a sense of security within and between states. These challenges transcend the national boundaries of individual states and cannot be addressed effectively by individual members. Organized crime, for instance, a rampant problem in this region, knows no national boundaries.

In addition, war in one country can often have a disastrous consequence not only on the national economy of the warring country but on the economies of the neighboring countries as well. The emergence of the SADC as a security community could be placed within such context (Schalkwyk 2005). According to Denis Venter (1996, 134) and Lloyd Ching'ambo (1992) in their analyses of regional security in southern Africa, the idea of collective security, in its traditional meaning, rarely offers peace in the developing world. Their rationale is based on the importance of nonmilitary internal and regional factors on the destabilization of regimes and societies in these parts of the world.

Headquartered in Gaborone, Botswana, the SADC is a regional bloc of fifteen member states[4], created originally to advance socioeconomic integration as well as political and security cooperation among its member states. The origins of the institution of the SADC go back to the 1960s and 1970s, when the political leaders and the national liberation movements in the southern African region coordinated their political, diplomatic and military struggles to bring an end to the Apartheid system in the region. These actions culminated with the creation of The Southern African Development Coordination Conference (SADCC) in July 1981. On August 17, 1992, the SADCC was transformed into the Southern African Development Community (SADC). The major innovation of the new institution was its combination of socioeconomic, political as well as its strong new emphasis of the security component. In the aftermath of South Africa's first free and fair elections in 1994, it became clear that the integration mechanisms of the Apartheid era needed to be closed in favor of a more forward-looking integration design.

The second major change in the institutional design of the SADC would take place on August 14, 2001, with the amendment of the 1992 version of the SADC treaty. Such amendment ushered in a new era which took a significant new step in the process of institutionalizing a security mechanism for the southern African region. The most prominent sign of such process resides in the creation of the Organ on Politics, Defense and Security (OPDS) (Ngoma 2005, 183). As one of the main bodies of the SADC, its primary function is to guarantee collective and common security by identifying common threats and collectively resolving to meet potential security challenges in the region (Ngoma 2005, 146). Thus, as Gabriël Oosthuizen explains, the OPDS constitutes the SADC's most important structure that has been associated with the promotion of peace and security in southern Africa. The objectives of the OPDS include, inter alia, the peaceful prevention, containment and resolution of inter- and intra-state conflict resorting to the use of military enforcement, if necessary (Oosthuizen 2006, 213).

These latest reforms have resulted in an institutional framework designed to cope with the new challenges that the region faces. The principal institutions of the Community, which resulted from the 2001 Summit, include at least ten major organs. The first major organ is the Summit, which is composed of heads of state and governments. The Summit is the decision and policy-making

---

4   The member states of SADC include Angola, Botswana, the Democratic Republic of the Congo, Lesotho, Madagascar, Malawi, Mauritius, Mozambique, Namibia, Seychelles, South Africa, Swaziland, United Republic of Tanzania, Zambia and Zimbabwe.

institution of the SADC. It meets annually and is headed by the chairperson of the SADC. The second major organ is the Troika, which is charged with the responsibility of executing tasks and implementing decisions expeditiously as well as providing policy direction to the SADC Institutions in the periods between regular SADC meetings. The third organ, which is arguably the most important in terms of it effect on security issues, is the Organ on Politics, Defense and Security (OPDS).

The fourth organ is the Council of Ministers, which is composed of ministers from each member state and is entrusted with the responsibility of overseeing the functioning and development of the SADC and ensuring that policies are properly implemented. The fifth organ is the Integrated Committee of Ministers whose main purpose is to provide proper policy guidance, coordination and harmonization of cross-sector activities in a variety of areas. The sixth organ is the Tribunal whose purpose is to adjudicate disputes and ensure adherence to, and proper interpretation of, the provisions of the SADC Treaty and its subsidiary instruments.

The seventh major organ is the SADC National Committees made of key stakeholders of the SADC, notably governments, private sectors and civil societies in member states. Their purpose is to give inputs in the formulation of regional policies, strategies, the SADC Program of Action (SPA) as well as coordinate and oversee the implementation of these programs at the national level. These committees are also responsible for initiating projects and issuing papers that provide input for the preparation of the Regional Indicative Development Plan.

The eighth major organ of the SADC is the Standing Committee of Senior Officials whose main purpose is to provide advice to the Councils of Ministers. It is made of one Permanent/Principal Secretary or an official of equivalent rank from each member state. The Chairperson and Vice-Chairperson of the Standing Committee are appointed from the member states holding the Chairpersonship and Vice-Chairpersonship, respectively, of the Council. The ninth organ of the SADC is the Secretariat, which, as the major executive institution, is primarily responsible for strategic planning, coordination and management of SADC programs. The SADC Standing Committee is also headquartered in Gaborone, Botswana, and is headed by an Executive Secretary. Finally, the structure of the SADC also includes Commissions and Sector Coordinating Units (SCUs) designed for the smooth functioning of the institution.

In sum, although the SADC has undergone impressive changes, as we discussed above, its structural organization reflects the worries of its founders—founders who were particularly aware of previous experiments with regional integration in Africa, some of which (namely the OAU) resulted in failure and disenchantment. In this respect, the current framework of the SADC is designed to avoid similar pitfalls. Thus, for instance, by putting a special emphasis on a decentralized institutional arrangement that would ensure that member states are the principal actors in the formulation and implementation of policy decisions, the SADC seeks to avoid the operational problems associated with the appearance that decisions to intervene in any circumstances could be the result of unilateral actions from any particular state.

Chapter 4

The Emergence of The African Union and The Limits of The Paradigms of International Politics

"**W**e are starting a new chapter in the history of our continent [...] Our people expect the changes to which we are committed [and] the rest of the world waits hopefully to see us do the things we hope to do" (Mbeki 2002). These were the words of President Thabo Mbeki of South Africa as forty African heads of state and governments gathered in Durban, South Africa, on July 8, 2002, to consecrate the birth of a security community. In reply to Mbeki's words, the then Secretary General of the United Nations, Koffi Annan, himself a native of Africa, had the following to say: "Your new determination to build peace and security must be felt when it matters most—and it matters now" (Annan 2004). Did the world take notice of this monumental development in Africa's history? Or did it simply shrug its shoulders as if to signal that what happened that day was nothing more than an additional gimmick, the kind which the rest of the world has, unfortunately, come to expect from the young nations of Africa in their search for a magic formula for a collective security mechanism?[1] That the world did not take notice could be a benign act. But that the rich and diversified theories of international relations did not predict the emergence of Africa's largest security community might be unconscionable. In this chapter, my main goal is to test liberal, realist and constructivist theories against the African experience

---

1 The African Union replaced the Organization of African Unity (OAU) which, at its birth, generated an extraordinary amount of hope only to prove a failure.

in order to determine whether the case of the African Union as a security community is consistent with the theoretical underpinnings of these three major theories of international relations.

Such security communities in the African case also include the Economic Community of West African States (ECOWAS) and the Southern Africa Development Community (SADC). For the purposes of this chapter, however, our attention will be focused on the case of the African Union for two essential reasons. The first is related to its size and the fact that the African Union encompasses the members of all other African security communities including ECOWAS and the SADC. The second reason is related to the relative youth of the African Union and the subsequent absence of detailed studies on the institution. Like Africa's major regional institutions, the African Union mainly comprises a security, a political and an economic dimension. These three dimensions are inextricably linked in the African context. However, because of the weakness of economic and political integration in Africa, the security dimension of the union tends to take a greater prominence. In this direction, the African Union's current security missions in Somalia (AMISOM) and Sudan (AMIS), to name but these most salient cases, highlights both the timeliness and the ripeness of a study of the continental organization. In this chapter, our focus will be directed on such security aspects of the African Union.

The case of the African Union constitutes a theoretical puzzle. Created in 2002, the African Union offers a unique opportunity to test the theories. Such a test is worthwhile for one essential theoretical reason. Much of international relations theories remain characterized by Eurocentric perspectives. Thus, beyond the immense theory-testing opportunities, an examination of the African experience has the potential to contribute something significant to our understanding of international relations. In the logic of Van Evera, our main intention is to peruse the case of the African Union in an attempt to determine whether events unfold in the manner in which the theories predict (Van Evera 1997, 29). In addition, since the three theories give diverging accounts of the emergence of security communities, the African Union, a novel security community, provides us with the opportunity to submit these various theoretical assumptions to close scrutiny in order to determine the degree to which they could be useful in their accounts.

In this respect, this chapter is a theoretical attempt to account for the emergence of particular regional institutions, especially those institutions that form security communities. In doing so, our aim is to specifically assess the major theoretical arguments on security communities. Most specifically, it is an attempt to explain the emergence of the African Union as a security community in the light of such theories. In this study, the concept of security community will be understood in the sense in which Deutsch referred to it. According to Deutsch, a security community can be defined as a group of people that has become integrated to the point that there is a "real assurance that the members of that community will not fight each other physically, but will settle their disputes in some other way" (Deutsch 1957, 5).

I. The African Union: Genesis of the Emergence of a Security Community

The emergence of the African Union as a security community can be understood as a combination of external and internal factors. It is often argued that the fall of the Berlin Wall opened a new era in international politics. The same is true for African politics. The symbolic event of November 9, 1989, in the capital city of Germany, indeed, ushered African politics into a new era. The collapse of the Soviet Bloc played a crucial role in the emergence of the African Union in the sense that it meant a decrease in the direct meddling of external powers into Africa's internal affairs.

Most importantly, it also meant that Africa's security would, first and foremost, be Africa's business. In this respect, the African Union was set up to overcome the security dilemma, which threatened the survival and well-being of African states. It was created to complement and reinforce existing regional security communities such as ECOWAS in West Africa and the SADC in southern Africa. ECOWAS, for instance, did set of the Economic Community of West African States Monitoring Group or ECOMOG, a West African multilateral armed force, designed to work along similar lines to NATO with Nigeria as its main provider.

The African Union fits into Deutsch's definition of a pluralistic security community. In Deutsch's views, a pluralistic security community is different from an amalgamated security community; amalgamated security communities merge their institutions whereas pluralistic security communities retain their respective legal sovereignties (Deutsch et al. 1957, 6–7). In addition, the fact that intrastate wars have virtually disappeared in Africa is consistent with Deutsch's theory. In this respect, the Durban summit of July 8, 2002, which consecrated the birth of the African Union, must be understood within these broad economic, political and security parameters. These three parameters form an intrinsic whole in the context of Africa. In this chapter, our main interest lies within the security parameter; in the case of Africa, the security parameter constitutes the building block for the economic and political parameters.

Such security parameter within the Union was consecrated on December 26, 2003, with the official ratification of the Protocol Related to the Peace and Security Council (PSC) of the African Union. In this direction, as its constitution stipulates, the African Union was established "to promote peace, security and stability on the continent" (Constitution of the AU 2002, available online at http://www.africa-union.org). This security protocol, whose main purpose is the creation of a zone of security among all member states, constitutes one of the strongest elements in the establishment of the African Union as a security community. In this respect, Gompert's (2006) comparative analysis of NATO and the African Union lends some strength to the argument that the emergence of the African Union obeys the logic of a security community. Thus his argument reinforces the notion that the African Union should look upon NATO as a partner and as a model for force planning and force generation.

The idea of a security union in Africa, however, can be traced back to the 1960s, which corresponds to the independence of most African countries.

When Ghana became the first sub-Saharan African country to free itself from the British yoke on March 6, 1957, its leader, Kwame Nkrumah, took a strong stand for the liberation of all of Africa and expressed the idea of a continental government as an amalgamated security community. This idea was carried on by African leaders such as Gamal Abdel Nasser of Egypt and Patrice Lumumba of the Congo-Kinshasha, as well as Julius Nyerere of Tanzania and Haile Selassie of Ethiopia.

In the beginning of the second millenary, the same idea of an African community was revived mainly by five modern African leaders: Muammar Khaddafi of Libya, Thabo Mbeki of South Africa, Olusegun Obasango of Nigeria, Abdel Aziz Bouteflika of Algeria and Abdoulaye Wade of Senegal. The idea of the union, a coalition of fifty-three states, was first emitted in official terms during the Syrte summit in Libya in September 1999 when Khaddafi proposed a United States of Africa. Such an idea received wide support on the part of the African leaders who were present at the 37th OAU summit July 2001 in Lusaka, Zambia. Support for the union was also clear in the then UN Secretary General's "tribute to leader [Khaddafi] for spearheading this development" (Annan 2004).

Within the context of the literature about security communities, the emergence of the African Union raises an interesting theoretical question. Do major theoretical traditions such as liberalism, constructivism and realism account for the emergence of the African Union? Such a question is critically important with respect to the conditions under which the African Union emerged. Why did Mbeki, Obansanjo, Bouteflika and Wade, the champions of good governance and democratic principles, follow Khaddafi who does not share their basic philosophies of government? How was it possible that the Group of Eight (G8), a coalition of the world's leading democracies, accepted to back up a project launched by a leader who, by their standards, is nothing more than a ruthless dictator and an international outcast? These are some considerations that this chapter will attempt to tackle.

II. The Liberal Paradigm

The liberal position on the development of security communities can be understood in terms of the logical outcomes of states engaging other states. In other words, as Karl Deutsch explains, states can engage in a set of social relations that are understood as a community, and the fabric of this community can generate stable expectations of peaceful change (Deutsch et al. 1957). In this section, our analysis of the liberal position will be twofold. First, we will examine briefly the major arguments of the liberal peace theory. Second, we will peruse the arguments of Karl Deutsch.

The liberal peace argument is premised on the notion that democracies speak peace with each other because they share a "liberal conscience" (Howard 1978, 70). Under this assumption, states that form a security community share a collective identity of democratic values, which in turn constitutes a powerful inhibition tool against any state's belligerent dispositions. This position could also be summed up in a succinct manner using Michael Williams' assessment of Kant's contributions to the literature. Williams' argument is structured around the idea that, as a theory, liberalism contains explanatory propositions with regards to the emergence of security communities. For him, the key lies with critically engaging with Immanuel Kant's elaboration of the democratic peace. Williams argues that Kantian liberalism contains subtle yet powerful processes of identity construction, and the processes of mutual recognition with which these identities are intertwined play essential constitutive and disciplining roles in the development of political relations.

In this respect, Kant's account of security communities is based on a shared democratic ideal among the states of a given community. Thus, using the case of NATO, Williams contends that such democratic security communities are structured around liberal identities and discipline (Williams 2001). In this direction, liberal theories of international relations in general and neoliberal institutionalism in particular accord a privileged place to the analysis of the liberal peace theory. The case of NATO, according to the liberal argument, is an illustration that the establishment of liberal institutions and norms is a factor of peace. Celeste Wallander's arguments converge along similar lines. In addition, she argues that security institutions are not merely created to cope with external threats. They also serve the purpose of addressing other crucial security problems such as instability, uncertainty and relations among allies (Wallander 2000, 706).

Arguing in the same vein, Benjamin Miller uses the cases of the Middle East, South America and Western Europe to show that peace and security is possible in any given region provided that three conditions are met. Such conditions operate at three levels: global, regional and domestic. They include (1) the presence of a great power hegemon or a great power concert which could enable the strategy of great power engagement, (2) the presence of strong and coherent states in the region which could facilitate the strategy of conflict resolution and (3) the presence of liberal democracies in the region which could facilitate the strategy of regional integration (Miller 2005).

However, the liberal argument regarding the emergence of security communities is dominated by the contributions of Karl Deutsch. Deutsch conceptualizes security communities in very succinct terms in his reference to Richard Van Wagenen's argument. "A security community," he says, "is considered to be a group which has become integrated, where integration is defined as the attainment of a sense of community, accompanied by formal or informal institutions or practices, sufficiently strong and widespread to assure peaceful change among members of a group with 'reasonable' certainty over a 'long' period of time" (Deutsch 1954, 33). Building on this concept, Deutsch argues that the presence or absence of a security community can be measured in terms of the presence or absence of significant organized preparations for war or large-scale violence among its members.

For Deutsch, the concept of community entails a group of countries that have a significant amount of transactions among them. In order for such communities to be political, there must exist the possibility of enforcement of decisions. And in order for such political communities to become security communities, there must a reasonable expectation of peace among the participating units or groups, regardless of whether or not there has been a merger of the political institutions of such groups. Integration, according to Deutsch, is the process by which habits and institutions are unified, and a security community is made of the territories and populations among which such integration takes place (Deutsch 1954, 33).

In a subsequent landmark study, Deutsch et al. (1957) identify two types of security communities. The first one is an amalgamated security community; the second one is a pluralistic security community. The difference between these two lies in the degree of amalgamation of their institutions. Thus, whereas the first one is characterized by unified and amalgamated institutions, the second one is characterized with few or no amalgamated institutions. With respect to the case of the African Union, our interest will be focused on the pluralistic security communities. The African Union fits into the category of pluralistic security communities since the institutions of African states have retained their sovereignties.

According to Deutsch, the existence of a pluralistic security community can be tested by "the absence of systematic advance preparation for warfare in terms of significant amounts of manpower and resources" (Deutsch 1954, 41). Most importantly, Deutsch et al. (1957) identifies a series of conditions that are essential to the emergence of a security community. Among such conditions, he identifies three that are essential for the emergence of both types of security communities. The first condition is shared values and expectations, the second essential condition is capabilities and communication processes, and the third mutual predictability of behavior. The extent to which these three conditions fit the case of the African Union will be examined in detail in this section.

But first, it may be worthwhile to point out that according to Deutsch (1954) the very idea of the emergence of security communities must be understood in terms of the necessity to fend off threats. In other words, a political community arises when smaller political units perceive major threats from within or from without. Once this security threat is perceived, smaller communities are replaced by larger ones (Deutsch 1954, 4). For Deutsch there is a link between a stable political integration and a stable security community. Such a link lies in the development and maintenance of adequate social institutions and habits of mutual response. This essential condition for any stable political integration is the pathway from political integration to a security community (Deutsch 1954, 45). Thus, in Deutsch's view, this link is cemented by a sense of community and mutual attention and responsiveness.

However, although the above-mentioned conditions may be necessary to the emergence of security communities, they may not be sufficient. Deutsch contends that the single most important condition for political integration and for the emergence of a stable security community in a given area may in fact be the distribution of autonomous political groups within it (Deutsch 1954, 49). Most specifically, three inherent factors of such distribution should be taken into account. The first is whether such autonomous groups are compatible. The second is the distribution and balance of the ranges of transaction among these autonomous groups. And the third is the volumes and dimensions of transactions. Together these three main clusters unfold into Deutsch's fourteen dimensions of integration. Most importantly, Deutsch contends that whether or not a security community will emerge out of a political community depends less on the sequence with which these fourteen dimensions come into existence than on the completeness and simultaneity with which these dimensions of political integration are all found in operation.

In addition, within the Deutschian paradigm, the concept of communication is central as a condition for the emergence of a security community. In other words, the level of communication that exists within a given community may determine whether a security community will emerge. This idea is especially prominent in his classic study of the North Atlantic Treaty Organization (NATO) as a model of security community. In this book, Deutsch and his coauthors define the idea of a community with reference to communication. For them, political communities are "social groups with a process of political communication, some machinery for enforcement and some popular habits of compliance" (Deutsch et al. 1957, 5). Most importantly, from the perspective of security communities, Deutsch and his collaborators argue that there is a relationship between the strength of the links of social communication and the strength of the integration between countries that compose a security community (Deutsch et al. 1957, 169).

Pushing their analysis further, they contend that some political communities are not able to prevent war and others are able to eliminate both war and the expectation of war within their boundaries. The latter cases are known as security communities and are the focus of Deutsch's analysis. Such security communities are divided into two groups. The first case is referred to as an amalgamated security community in which states formally unify. The second one is referred to as a pluralistic security community in which states retain their sovereignty. Both have dependable expectations of peaceful change. However, this idea of mutual expectations is not synonymous with a guarantee that two states within a security community will not go to war. It simply signifies that since nothing in the history of these two states shows a proclivity for such belligerent attitude, there should be a reasonable expectation that one state will not invade the other.

There are inherent strengths in Deutsch's theory when it is applied to the African experience. The most obvious one may lie in Deutsch's recognition of the centrality of elites in the development of security communities. The African Union is clearly a product of Africa's leadership, as we have argued in the first section of this chapter. In addition, the strength of Deutsch's theory can be measured in terms of Deutsch's second condition. As a security community, the African Union, just like ECOWAS and SADC, strengthens Deutsch's concept of capabilities and communication processes. Deutsch argues that the strength of such communication between the different political units that compose the community must be supported by some core states with markedly superior economic growth. Africa's security communities are mainly supported by Africa's two major economic giants: Nigeria in West Africa and South Africa in southern Africa.

However, the case of the African Union, just like the case of the other major African security communities (i.e., ECOWAS and the SADC), may constitute an insurmountable challenge for Deutsch and his collaborators in two of Deutsch's three major conditions. The first one is related to the concept of shared political and social values and expectations among the political elites. At this level it will suffice to point to the fact that among the five major leaders who spearheaded the African Union, the main architect is Khaddafi of Libya, whose political and social values differ fundamentally from those of Mbeki of South Africa or Obasanjo of Nigeria. Yet despite these essential political differences at the elite level in these states, the African Union emerged.

As for the third condition, mutual predictability of behavior, it illustrates the limits of Deutsch's theory in accounting for security communities in Africa. At the core of Deutsch's theory, as illustrated by his Scandinavian example, lies the idea that the absence of a history of invasions makes it a safe bet for Scandinavian countries to assume that the invasion of one Scandinavian country by another is highly unlikely. Yet, a recent history of Africa reveals that such a bet could not safely be made. Examples of aggressive behaviors between dyads of African countries pullulate. Nevertheless, the African Union, ECOWAS and the SADC emerged as security communities despite such a history.

Moreover, two problems could at the very least stem from explaining the African experience in light of the Deutschian paradigm. The first is that although interstate wars have become very rare in Africa, a different type of war has persisted despite the emergence of the African Union. In this respect, civil wars such as the ones in Ivory Coast, Liberia, Sierra Leone and the Congo could not be satisfactorily accounted for by Deutsch. The second is the leadership variable. Although Deutsch's theory recognizes the centrality of leadership in the development of security communities, it tends to subordinate the impact of leadership to his three conditions. And as we have just argued, two of those three conditions are violated in the African case.

Ultimately, for the liberals, shared political and social values along with a history of reliable and predictable behavior constitute essential conditions for the emergence of security communities. In addition, what binds Deutsch and his liberal colleagues is their conviction that the emergence of security communities is tied to the democratic principle. Under the liberal assumption, states that share this fundamental principle are thus more likely to create a security community.

III. The Constructivist Paradigm

The constructivist approach contains striking similarities with the liberal position. This is especially true if we take into consideration constructivist accounts of the causal factors of security communities. An understanding of the constructivist account of the emergence of security communities is not possible without an understanding of the core assumptions that underlie this specific tradition. Such assumptions could be understood with reference to the origins of constructivism. The origins of the constructivist tradition could be traced back to the thoughts of the Italian philosopher Giambattista Vico. For Vico, the natural environment is a creation of God, but the historical setting is man's creation. In other words, men make all history and all historical constructs, including the state system and the international system. For the constructivists, the international system is a set of ideas, a system of norms created by a given people for a particular purpose. Seminal in their system of thought is the notion of time and place as well as process. In other words, such norms and ideas can undergo processes of changes. And such changes in identities, norms and beliefs shape the behavior of nation-states.

In this respect, the emergence of a security community can be understood in terms of changes in ideas, norms and processes. This is especially true since, for the constructivists, there is no external or objective social reality. They argue that the international system, along with the institutions that allow it to function, is not an independent reality all by itself. Instead, it is a purely intellectual and ideational product of human creativity, not an objective reality. Alexander Wendt's (1992) articulation of social structures and processes constitutes an invaluable contribution to the debate as it relates to both such processes and norms. For Wendt, the emergence of social structures is predicated upon some shared understandings, expectations or knowledge within a given community.

In this sense, Wendt perceives a security dilemma as a social structure in which the distrust among states is significant to the extent that each of them makes the worst-case assumptions about the other's intentions. This, in turn, results in a self-help anarchic system. The opposite of a security dilemma in Wendt's view is a security community, which emerges out of shared understanding, knowledge and expectations. Most importantly, a security community is different from a security dilemma in the sense that in a security community there is a trust among states—leading to a peaceful resolution of conflicts before they evolve into war. In this sense, like liberalism and unlike realism, the constructivist tradition carries an idealist explanation for the emergence of a security community.

In addition, Wendt views the international system in general, and its institutions in particular, as products of our consciousness. In Wendt's views, as in those of Peter Katzenstein (1996), Friedrich Kratochwil (1989) and Nicholas Onuf (1989), the concept of consciousness holds a central place. This runs counter to Waltz and the positivist argument of the neorealists. In fact, Wendt's argument, to a large extent, constitutes a critical assessment of the neorealist assumptions. Whereas neorealists in the mold of Waltz argue in favor of the primacy of structure over process, Wendt is convinced to the contrary. In other words, he maintains that the anarchic and self-help nature of international politics is a product of process not of structure. This tendency to value process and identity as an explanatory variable over structure is widely shared by constructivists. Jepperson et al. (1996, 62) construct their study around the idea that identity trumps geostrategy in the creation of security communities. For them, the fact that Israel is closer to the community of Western democracies than to her Arab neighbors constitutes the prime example that security alliances are a function of identity not geostrategy. In addition, the fact that, as a security community, NATO emerged out of an alliance between Western

Europe and the United States instead of between the latter and the Soviet Union (Risse-Kappen 1996) constitutes yet an additional case for their argument.

Thus, in general, the idea of change and transformation in global politics as the result of changes in social processes is essential in constructivist accounts of security communities. For the constructivists, such global changes, which lead to the emergence of security communities, depend on evolving epistemic and normative interpretations of the material world (Risse-Kappen 1996; Wendt 1994). John Ruggie's (1998) contributions abound in the same direction and are structured around three core ideas. Whereas the first two fit the African experience, the third idea can be open to discussion.

First, he argues that the existence of core states is a sine qua non for the emergence of a security community. He illustrates his argument with historic cases both at the national level (Prussia in the process of German unification in the nineteenth century and Piedmont in Italy) and at the international level (Sweden in the pluralistic Scandinavian community and the United States in the transatlantic organization). In the case of the African Union, such core states comprise Nigeria to the west and South Africa to the south. Second, citing the examples of the North Atlantic Treaty Organization, he contends that security communities follow and complement economic and cultural ties of the member states (Ruggie 1998, 231). In other words, to understand why security communities emerge, we must take into account the broader dynamics of economic, political and cultural settings. For him such economic integration constitutes the necessary condition, and the security mechanism is the sufficient condition for integration. Finally, while acknowledging the inherent difficulties to determine the exact causal mechanisms that lead to the emergence of a security community, he suggests that external threats from the Soviet Union in the case of NATO may be the single most decisive factor. Nevertheless other factors such as economic integration, common bonds in civil society, market economy and constitutional democracy have also played their part. In sum, Ruggie's argument shares in the concept that the social construction of security communities is a function of shared identities and internalized beliefs.

Finally, the constructivist analysis of the emergence of security communities is highly reconcilable with the liberal perspective. In this respect, although Thomas Risse-Kappen's analysis, for instance, is centered on the democratic peace argument, he offers a constructivist variety of the same essential liberal argument. For him, democracies are more likely to form pluralistic security communities because they perceive in each other a predisposition for peace. This shared collective identity is what makes democracies particularly predisposed to form international institutions that are aimed at consolidating the peace among democracies (Risse-Kappen 1995, 37). Emmanuel Adler and Michael Barnett's argument constitutes another illustration of the grey area separating the two traditions of constructivism and liberalism in their accounts of the emergence of security communities.

They contend that communities emerge when actors sharing common values, norms, and symbols that provide a social identity start interacting. For them, such interactions reflect long-term interest, diffuse reciprocity and trust. In this respect, they argue that a community exists at the international level and that security politics is profoundly shaped by it. In addition, they maintain that "those states dwelling within an international community might develop a pacific disposition" toward each other (Adler and Barnett 1998, 1). In other words, Adler and Barnett perceive a reinforcing interaction effect between the twin concepts of security and community. Nicholas Onuf's discussion of security regimes (1989, 150) could be understood in such light. He argues that the formalization of international rules both within and among states could also develop a peaceful predisposition between the different states that eventually form a security community. To what extent does the constructivist paradigm account for the case of the African Union? This question will be analyzed in the last section of this chapter.

IV. The Realist Paradigm

The realist perspective on this issue is particularly interesting because, although realism does not deal directly with the concept of security community, the question of security itself is a key concept in realist theories both among the classical realists and the structural realists. In this respect, an exploration of the realist tradition is a legitimate one.

Among all three theories of international relations under review, realism is the theory that seems to deal the least with the question of security communities. In fact, there is no explicit realist theory of security communities, and the concept of "security community" is not of common usage among political realists. For instance, neither the works of Morgenthau nor those of Waltz, two major realist thinkers, make an explicit mention of the concept. This may seem rather surprising considering the fact that, as a philosophical tradition, political realism deals extensively with the concept of security. However, this lack of explicit consideration for the concept may be explained by the fact that the realist tradition is grounded on the reliance on individual states to overcome the security dilemma. In his analysis of the post–Cold War security arrangements in Europe, for instance, John Mearsheimer (1994/1995) contends that the rejection of power politics as an organizing concept is essentially both misguided and dangerous. For him, the promise of what he regards as the three major institutionalist theories (liberalism, collective security, and critical theories) about regional peace through the development of regional institutions is false, mainly because the causal logic of these theories is flawed.

Nevertheless, realists agree with constructivists and liberals that institutions do operate at the international level. They also share the idea, and this is especially true with regards to Deutsch, that such institutions are usually sustained by the most powerful states within the community. However, the bone of contention between realism on one hand and liberalism and constructivism on the other hand lies within what they perceive to be the causal mechanisms that lead to the emergence of security communities. Whereas Deutsch argues that institutional arrangements such as security communities arise out of shared identities and values, the realists claim that such institutions emerge out of the desire of the most powerful states to maintain and even increase their share of power. For this reason, Mearsheimer argues against the idea that the security of Europe during the Cold War was the result of the emergence of NATO. Instead, he contends the real cause of Europe's Peace and stability during the Cold War was the bipolar distribution of power in Europe. For him, NATO is only an intervening variable in this relationship (Mearsheimer 1994/1995, 14). In addition, realists argue that to the extent that such individual states need alliances to overcome the security dilemma, such alliances are only temporary and would disappear when the threats disappear (Mearsheimer 1990; Waltz 1979).

Yet, despite its apparent lack of direct take on the issue, no serious study of security communities could exist without considering realist theories for at least two essential reasons. The first one is related to realism's focus on understanding the crucial issues of war and peace. The realist idea of security alliances, which are created to overcome the security dilemma, constitutes too important a contribution in the debate to be ignored. In this respect, realism constitutes an interesting framework from which to analyze the conditions necessary for the emergence of security communities. In this vein, Robert Jervis's analysis of the conditions that lead to the creation of alliances constitutes a valuable starting point. He argues that cooperation is more likely when the gains from mutual cooperation and the costs of noncooperation are high. In addition, he contends, like Waltz, that the influence of geography is crucial to the creation of security alliances (Jervis 1978).

The second and most important reason may be related to the nature of the particular security community under review in this chapter. In this respect, taking into account the fact that the other two major theories of security communities, namely liberalism and constructivism, only explain partial pieces of the African puzzle, an exploration of the realist tradition may contribute something essential to the scholarship. This is all the more legitimate since the case of the African Union seems to obey some essential realist tenets. In the words of Robert Keohane (1986, 7) realism contains three key assumptions. The first assumption is that realists take the state (or city-states) as their unit of analysis. The second assumption is that states seek power either as an end in itself or as a means to other ends. The final assumption is that, overall, states behave in rational ways. Most importantly, for the purpose of this study, we should note that realist thinkers share the pessimistic view that, in a system in which the major purpose of sovereign states is survival and the maximization of power, states often resort to power politics (Thucydides 431 BC; Hobbes 1651; Morgenthau 1948).

Thus, taking realists perspectives into account, the concept of security among states must be analyzed within the broader context of power. For the realists, power politics accounts for peace. In this sense, a security community within the framework of realism could be viewed as nothing more than an aggregation of national power and purpose. In other words, the development of security communities may be less a function of shared values and identities, as the liberals and constructivists contend, than a product of states intent upon guaranteeing their security by using the organization as a tool. This seems to fit the African case. Otherwise how could we account for the creation of the

African Union as a security community despite the diverging identities and values of its member states? Most baffling, how was it possible for the African Union, an idea launched by a known detractor of the democratic values of governance and an "international outcast," to get the backing of the champions of good governance and even the Group of Eight (G8), whose members are among the world's major democracies?

This fact in itself illustrates all the complexities of international politics and seems to obey the logic of realism. Our contention is that the champions of good governance joined in the proposal of Khaddafi as a result of a cost-benefits analysis and "realpolitik." The African Union, in a purely African context, is a marriage of convenience not of love. Mbeki, Obasanjo, Bouteflika and Wade joined with Khaddafi to set up the African Union not out of shared identity and values but out of shared interests. Otherwise, how is it comprehensible that these leaders would join Khaddafi whose blasts at the democratically elected African leaders as the puppets of the Western system are widely known? In this respect, the African Union's decision to retrieve the African Peer Review Mechanism (APRM) could be read as a measure to accommodate Khaddafi. The APRM was primarily aimed at promoting democratic principles of government within Africa.

As for the G8, their support for this African initiative could be seen as a means to contribute to international security—and to their security own by ricochet. The invocation of moral obligations may just be a self-satisfying device. The G8's support for the African Union, despite identity and value differences, is especially relevant in the context of a post–9/11 world. Helping the African continent cope with its insecurity problems constitutes a realistic measure for the G8 countries to help themselves by using the African Union as a domestic tool in the war for global security. The weakness of African institutions in this era is not only an African problem; it has become a grave threat to global security. In this sense, the emergence of the African Union along with the support of the G8 countries, particularly the United States, could be interpreted in terms of their realization that African institutions must be made stronger in order to prevent the spread of international insecurity. The case of Somalia and of so many other failed states and weak states that pullulate in Africa is perceived as a threat not only to Africa's security but to the security of the rest of the world.

This argument is all the more legitimate since failed or weak states could constitute sanctuaries for terrorists groups. The case of Sudan, which harbored Osama Bin Laden, the leader of al-Qaeda, could constitute a perfect illustration. In this respect, the creation of the African Union could also be read in terms the G8's support as an effort to create a tool for its own security. This fact constitutes a fit to Mearsheimer's offensive realism. Mearsheimer (2001) argues that, in an anarchic world, the dominant state must not only maximize its power, it must also take offensive measures designed for its own security. In this case, such offensive measures include using international institutions as a tool geared toward achieving its own security. In this direction, the fact that the African Union is taking steps in combating international terrorism in the aftermath of 9/11 (Ewi and Aning 2006) reinforces this notion.

Strong as the realist perspective might be, it contains, however, one major fault. Although the power politics argument is not devoid of meaning in the African context, it does not provide the only explanation for the emergence of the African Union. As we have argued above, the African union is the product of a variety of factors, some of which extend beyond the simple concept of power politics.

V. The Emergence of the African Union and the Limits of the Paradigms of International Politics

This chapter has analyzed three major philosophical traditions that address the issue of the role of institutions in international peace. In this sense, our main goal was to attempt to provide new insights from the particular perspective of the African Union. Liberalism, constructivism, and realism all address this uniquely important question. They do so with similarities as well as differences both in their approaches and outcomes. Each of these three approaches explains parts of this puzzle. But in the case of the African Union, realism, with all its limitations, seems to provide better explanations nonetheless. For a variety of reasons, the liberal and constructivist accounts are also only partially useful in explaining the emergence of the African Union as a security community. Their basic contention that security communities arise out of the need to overcome the security dilemma is well grounded. However, their accounts are faced with two major difficulties when applied to the African case.

The first among such difficulties is their account of the nature of the security dilemma that makes it necessary for a security community to spring up. In their analysis, the focus is on external factors. In other words, their arguments rest on the notion that security communities are created as a remedy for the interstate security dilemma. In this respect, their major fault is having ignored the intrastate variable. The African Union is the perfect illustration that security communities are also created out of different needs. They can be born out of the need to protect the state from the state, the need to protect the citizens from their own states and the need to protect some citizens from other citizens within the same states. In addition, they can rise out of the general need to protect citizens of failed states. The permanent state of crisis in many African states (e.g., Somalia, Liberia, and Sierra Leone) brought Africa's leadership to the realization that a mechanism is needed for policing the civil wars that impact almost the entire continent. In addition, as we have previously argued, the G8's support for the creation of the African union also obeys the logic of self-protection, especially in a post-9/11 international environment.

The second major problem is related to the processes that lead to the emergence of security communities. The constructivist paradigm's focus on process over structure constitutes a major fault in the case of the African Union. Although both the constructivists and the neorealists agree on the basic notion that anarchy explains the emergence of security communities or security alliances, they disagree on the mechanisms and processes that lead to their emergence. In this respect, whereas the constructivists argue that the emergence of a security community is determined less by the structure of the system than by process, the realists argue the opposite. A careful analysis of the condition under which the African Union was created, however, reveals that the critical element may be determined less by process than by structure. On this particular account, one should note that although the emergence of the African Union as a security community is an obvious result of a "process," there is no evidence to suggest, in this case, that process holds a greater sway than structure. The contiguous nature of the borders of this union seems to be the decisive factor in the emergence of the African Union. In other words, the geographical structure of the African countries that form the security community seems to be more important than the process—such a process may not have been possible in the absence of this existing structural reality. This is all the more legitimate since the very membership in this union is solely based on belonging to a given continent.[2] In this sense, the African Union differs fundamentally from the transatlantic organization, or the European Union for that matter, in the sense that membership is not necessarily determined by shared democratic principles and values.

For this reason, the idea that identity trumps geostrategy (Jepperson et al. 1996, 62) may be problematic in the African context. A security community in which all members belong to the same continent calls for a legitimate revision of such a theoretical argument. But this does not take away the fact that the constructivist position has some merits in a variety of cases, including, as they contend, the case of Israel—a country situated in the heart of the Middle East yet remaining a security partner to Western democracies precisely because of a shared identity. However, the African experience structured around one continental entity shows that such an argument may not be transportable.

As for the liberal/realist divide, the divergence can be located mainly at the level of the conditions that each theory perceives to be sine qua non. Thus while the liberals argue that shared democratic values are critically important, the realists point to power politics as the determinant variable. The emergence of the African Union amidst a lack of shared identities and values (e.g., democratic identity) may constitute the biggest weapon for the realist argument. If anything, the case of the African Union shows that structure (i.e., geostrategy) trumps identity and values in the emergence of security communities. This fact does not signify that political realism provides a satisfactory explanation for the emergence of the African Union. Realism's focus on power politics as an explanatory variable faces its own limits. As the African case illustrates. there is a complexity of the factors at play in the emergence of security communities.

---

2   Morocco is the only African State that has not joined the union. Morocco refuses to join because of the admission of the Sahrawi Arab Democratic Republic (SADR), which Morocco still considers as an integral part of its territory.

VI. Conclusion

Bruce Russett (1993, 42) contended that all the empirical work in international politics to date has employed modern and westernized definitions of both war and democracy, and he called for the need to revisit these definitions for more insights about the relative importance of normative and institutional constraints. The case of the African Union shows the benefits that might come from such a novel approach in the sense that the African experiment constitutes an illustration that security communities may not necessarily be a function of shared identities and expectations. They may also emanate partly from realpolitik. In this respect, the neorealist argument that international and domestic environments are largely devoid of cultural and institutional elements and therefore are best captured by materialist imagery like the balance of power or bureaucratic politics is one that seems to partially capture the African experience.

In sum, this study shows that all three traditional theories of international politics fit the African case only partially. However, the counterintuitive finding of this study resides in the fact that although liberalism and constructivism provide more elaborate theories of security communities in general, realism seems to offer the closest explanation to the "African puzzle." The creation of security communities in Africa is less a function of the nature of the regimes than it is a function of the nature of state interests. As Farber and Gowa (1997) put it, common interest, not common polities, might be more useful in explaining the peace among nations. The same may well be true for Africa.

However, although the evidence might seem to tilt in favor of a realist account of the emergence of security communities in Africa, realism alone does not satisfactorily account for the emergence of the African Union. In this direction, one might gain from taking into account Norrin Ripsman's insights. Building from the case of Western Europe in the aftermath of the Second World War, his argument reconciles the liberal and realist positions on this issue. For him, liberal mechanisms and institutions are necessary to sustain and strengthen regional peace. But the emergence of such a peace in a given region is a function of political realism (Ripsman 2005).

In other words, security communities emerge in the first place when states decide to put their differences aside and cooperate on the basis of realistic expectations. Yet, the endurance of such security communities is better captured by the liberal and constructivist perspectives—they are better able to explain the strengthening process that such security communities must undergo to remain viable institutions. In sum, although all three theories contain inherent strengths in their accounts, none of them explains satisfactorily the emergence of the African Union as a security community. If anything, the case of the African Union underscores the limits of the traditional theories of international politics, which remain bounded into fixed Eurocentric assumptions.

Chapter 5

The Emergence of ECOWAS and The Limits of The Paradigms of International Politics

Following the spirit of the preceding chapter, our main goal in this chapter is to test the three major paradigms of international politics (liberalism, constructivism and realism) in order to determine their usefulness in explaining the emergence of the Economic Community of West African States (ECOWAS). As we discussed in the second chapter, ECOWAS was founded in 1975 and is a regional organization of fifteen countries[1] with the defined mission of integrating West African states. Its original goals and objectives are explicit in its Article 3, which states, "[t]he aims of the Community are to promote cooperation and integration, leading to the establishment of an economic union in West Africa in order to raise the living standards of its peoples, and to maintain and enhance economic stability, foster relations among Member States and contribute to the progress and development of the African Continent" (The Treaty of ECOWAS, available online at http://www.ecowas.int). In sum, ECOWAS was born out of the realization that the individual domestic markets of West African states could not, with respect to their sizes, be competitive in an international environment characterized by the existence of large trade blocs. However, with the increasing awareness that these goals can only be met within the confines

---

1   The fifteen member states of ECOWAS are Benin, Burkina Faso, Cape Verde, Côte D'Ivoire, the Gambia, Ghana, Guinea, Guinea Bissau, Liberia, Mali, Niger, Nigeria, Senegal, Sierra Leone and Togo. Mauritania withdrew from ECOWAS in 2002.

of a secured community, ECOWAS has progressively adjusted its constitution to incorporate a paramount security dimension into the organization. Such evolution will be discussed in greater detail in the next section of this chapter.

At this point, it will suffice to point out that the problems associated with the lack of security within a number of states in West Africa constitute a top priority for all the governments in the region. According to Abubakar Momoh (2000), not a single West African country is entirely free of some sort of violent conflict. Such conflicts are present in Burkina Faso with its human rights abuses. They also include Senegal, with the deepening crisis in its southern region of Casamance, and Côte d'Ivoire, where the unrest after the coup of December 1999 has not completely been settled (with ensuing carnage in the aftermath of the election of Alassane Ouattara in 2011). In Guinea Bissau the events that led to the deposing of President Nino Vieira on May 10, 1999, have caused carnage and civil war. Such crises also include Togo, where the transfer of power from a deceased father to a son was vehemently contested in 2005 and has yet to be fully accepted. Finally, the crises also include Nigeria, where the oil-minority question and separatist agitations are still unresolved. In Nigeria such thorny issues also involve unresolved religious questions that occasionally disrupt the harmony of the Nigerian society. On April 14, 2014, the world watched with impotence and shock as 276 school girls were kidnapped from the Government Secondary School in Borno, Nigeria, by the extremist organization Boko Haram.

It is also important to note that, as serious as these crises might be, they pale in comparison to the senseless, large-scale and systematic massacre which took place in the context of total breakdown of sovereign authority in several West African states, including Liberia and Sierra Leone. ECOWAS, and later its monitoring group also known as the Economic Community of West African States Monitoring Group (ECOMOG), emerged in such context in an attempt to secure the West African region.

I. ECOWAS: Genesis of a Security Community

The institutional evolution of ECOWAS is different from that of the African Union. Originally, ECOWAS was founded for the purposes of the economic integration of West African states. However, in the aftermath of the collapse of the state in Liberia, following the outbreak of civil wars in that country in 1989, a consensus was beginning to emerge that ECOWAS needed to be transformed into a security community. In this direction, the charter of the organization was transformed to include the maintenance of regional security by including military intervention among its objectives (Talentino 2005, 71). Such transformation took place against concerns regarding the spillover effects of the Liberian conflict in the West African region.

These concerns have become all the more legitimate since the outbreak of the civil war in Liberia, which has been linked directly to the outbreak of war in neighboring Sierra Leone, with officials in Liberia involved at the highest level. This includes the former president of Liberia, Charles Taylor, who is today charged with war crimes in Liberia as well as Sierra Leone. These events largely explain the creation of the ECOWAS Monitoring Group (ECOMOG), the de facto military wing of ECOWAS that was created to overcome the security dilemma threatening the survival and well-being not only of Liberia but also of West African states at large. Since its emergence, ECOMOG has been called upon to deal with a variety of conflicts in West Africa. Such conflicts are mainly internal, with some cases of spillover. ECOMOG, a West African multilateral armed force designed to work along similar lines to NATO, was thus created to deal with this new kind of regional threat.

In this respect, the Liberian conflict has in fact ushered ECOWAS into a new era as a full-fledged security community in 1990. Although Article 4 of the 1975 ECOWAS Charter provides for collective security if the peace and security of a member state is threatened by an internal armed conflict that is supported by an external entity, subsequent constitutional transformations of the ECOWAS charter have gradually strengthened the security dispositions of the organization. Nowhere are such transformations more salient than in the revised ECOWAS Treaty of July 1993, which was inspired significantly by the Liberian conflict and signed in Cotonou, Benin. ECOWAS' 1993 Treaty puts the concerns of security front and center. Such concerns are clearly articulated in Article 4 in no uncertain terms and include

- nonaggression between member states;
- maintenance of regional peace, stability and security through the promotion and strengthening of good neighborliness; and
- peaceful settlement of disputes among member states, active cooperation between neighboring countries and promotion of a peaceful environment as a prerequisite for economic development.[2]

Such constitutional transformations were designed to enhance the organization's capacity to deal with the new security challenges that are emerging around the West African subregion. The dramatic mutation of ECOWAS into a security community, like the emergence of the African Union, must also be understood within the international context that made it necessary. The symbolic fall of the Berlin Wall and the end of the Cold War in 1989 have had profound implications in the international and domestic politics of African countries. West Africa is no exception in this respect. During their entire existence, generally in the 60s until the end of the Cold War, West African States have had to rely on the great power of the two blocs (West and East) for their security from internal strife. In return, both the Western and the Soviet Blocs vied for strategic influence in the young nation-states of Africa. As the Cold War ended, however, African states in general, and West African states in particular. ceased to play a strategic role—since one bloc had been defeated, it was no longer necessary for the West and the East to compete against each other for influence over Africa.

---

2   See the 1993 Treaty of ECOWAS, available online at http://www.comm.ecowas.int, accessed December 21, 2008.

Thus, the end of the Cold War has also translated into the erosion of the ability of African regimes to manipulate bipolar tensions for their own interests. Consequently, West African regimes and African regimes in general found themselves weaned off external support for their survival. The vacuum that has been left with the departure of Western and Eastern powers constitutes a background for understanding why it became increasingly necessary for West African states and African states in general to establish collective security mechanisms that they could control. In this respect, the major difference between the development of the African Union and ECOWAS as security communities is while the African Union was built from the remains of a defunct organization (i.e., the OAU) and included a security component from its inception, ECOWAS simply underwent major transformations in order to include a security component.

As in the case of Africa in general, however, the idea of a security mechanism in West Africa can be traced back to the birth of most African and West African nation-states in the beginning of the 1960s. The first expression of a community in West Africa emerged on April 4, 1959, in the form of the Mali Federation when the Republic of Senegal and the Republic of Mali (known at the time as the French Sudan) accepted merging their institutions into a single self-governing entity. This integration in the form of an amalgamated community was supposed to lay the groundwork for a greater community by concentric circles. Unfortunately, when Leopold S. Senghor, the president of Senegal, decided to withdraw from the union over political differences, he dashed all future hopes for an amalgamated community in the West African region.

Nigeria's federation constitutes another major and more successful case of an amalgamated community in West Africa. According to Rotimi Suberu (2005, 1), "Nigeria is arguably Africa's leading experiment in the building and remodeling of federalist institutions." For Suberu, since Nigeria's independence in 1960, the Nigerian federation has managed to evolve from a colonial federal legacy, which was based on three unwieldy component regions, into a greater union of 36 states and 774 constitutionally entrenched localities.

The case of ECOWAS, however, constitutes a decisive moment in the history of Africa in that, for the first time in its history, fully autonomous nation-states bequeathed a portion of their sovereignty to a subregional organization. The idea of a West African community goes back to President William Tubman of Liberia, who made the call in 1964 followed by the signing of an agreement between Côte d'Ivoire, Guinea, Liberia and Sierra Leone in February 1965. Tubman's efforts were fruitless, however. The decisive break came when, in April 1972, General Yakubu Gowon of Nigeria and General Gnassingbé Eyadéma of Togo relaunched the idea, drew up proposals and toured twelve countries, soliciting their plan from July to August 1973. In December of the same year, a meeting was called at Lomé to write a draft treaty. Their plan was further examined at different meetings in Accra in January 1974 and in Monrovia in January 1975. On May 28, 1975, in Lagos, Nigeria, fifteen West African countries signed the treaty for an Economic Community of West African States. A year later, on November 5, 1976, in Lomé, Togo, the protocols launching ECOWAS were signed (The Institute for Security Studies 2008, available at http://www.iss.org.za).

The most clear articulation of a security mechanism within the West African sub-region, however, can be traced back to May 29, 1981, when Nigeria, Ghana and other ECOWAS members agreed to a Protocol on Mutual Defense Assistance (PMDA) in Freetown, the capital city of Sierra Leone. The PMDA provided for the establishment of an Allied Armed Force of the Community (AAFC). The most decisive moment in the history of ECOWAS as a security community, however, coincidences with the institution of ECOMOG at the height of the Liberian civil war on August 25, 1990.

According to Margaret Vogt (1996, 166) the initial reason the ECOWAS Standing Mediation Committee (SMC) proposed the deployment of a monitoring force, ECOMOG, was to facilitate the rescue of civilians. This initial proposition was opposed by Charles Taylor, whose aim was to depose the regime of Samuel Doe as well as President Blaise Compaore of Burkina Faso. Charles Taylor argued that the main reason why ECOWAS existed was for economic purposes only and that ECOWAS had no business tackling security issues (The African Concord September 28, 1990). Despite such opposition, the decision to deploy ECOMOG was approved by consensus at the first ever extraordinary session of the Authority of Heads of State and Government held in Bamako, Mali, in November 1990. The decision was approved mainly because a good number of important members of the organization were sufficiently interested and committed to providing necessary support.

Vogt (1996, 167) argues that the institution of ECOMOG marks the first time a regional organization has mobilized the military forces of its member states for an extensive military operation designed to deal with a collective security problem. The rationale for the institution of ECOMOG was articulated in no uncertain terms by its main proponent, the Nigerian President Ibrahim Babangida, who contended that effective economic integration strategies could not be conducted amidst a security vacuum (Vogt 1996, 169). For Babangida (1990), effective economic interaction can best be conducted when there is full and effective security of life and property and freedom of movement of peoples. In an effort to match his words with his actions, President Babangida committed 10,000 soldiers to the operations, and paid more than three-quarters of the bills and made Nigeria the prime mover of ECOMOG (Vogt 1996, 167).

This major transformation caused by the total breakdown of sovereign authority in Liberia would ultimately lead to other momentous transformations in the institutional evolution of ECOWAS. One such transformation was occurred on December 10, 1999, which coincides with the adoption of the Protocol Relating to the Mechanism for Conflict Prevention, Management, Resolution, Peacekeeping and Security (the Mechanism) at Lomé, Togo. This protocol constitutes yet a major step in the consolidation of the security component of ECOWAS.

This new norm drew from the lessons learned from the ECOMOG experience that the concept of security is a sine qua non for the welfare of the populations of the West African subregion. Abass (2000), for instance, argues that the ratification of the Mechanism by member states of ECOWAS constitutes a major constitutional change toward a collective security system in the West African subregion. The Mechanism, according to Abass, departs clearly from the traditional principles of state sovereignty and empowers ECOWAS to intervene in the internal conflicts of member states. The provisions of the 1999 Mechanism depart clearly from those of the 1981 Protocol Relating to Mutual Assistance on Defence (PMAD), which remained attached to the principle of state sovereignty.

In its Article 18, the PMAD stipulated that "Community forces shall not intervene if the conflict remains purely internal." In contrast, the 1999 Mechanism stipulates clearly in its Article 40 that "ECOWAS shall intervene to alleviate the suffering of the populations and restore life to normalcy in the event of crises, conflict and disaster." It asserts further, "where the environment of a Member State is gravely devastated, appropriate steps shall be taken to rehabilitate it" (ECOWAS Constitution 1999, available online at http://www.ecowas.int). For these reasons, our test of the major paradigms of international politics will take into account both the emergence of ECOWAS as a community in general and the rise of ECOMOG, which marks the transformation of ECOWAS from a political and economic community to a security community. As Ero (2000, 2) explains, these transformations were aimed at expanding the mandate of ECOWAS from political and economic matters to that of managing, resolving and preventing conflicts.

Like the African Union, ECOWAS fits into Deutsch's definition of a pluralistic security community. In this respect, the Lagos summit of May 28, 1975, which consecrated the birth of ECOWAS, must be understood within these broad economic, political and security parameters. The institution of ECOMOG constitutes the final step in the evolution of ECOWAS as a security community. These three parameters form an inseparable entity in the context of Africa in general and West Africa in particular. In this chapter, our main interest lies within the security parameter in the sense that, in the case of West Africa, it constitutes the building block for the other two. Finally, it may be worthwhile to emphasize the role of Nigeria in the institution of both ECOWAS and ECOMOG. According to Mortimer (1996, 149), "most observers of the ECOMOG experience have emphasized Nigeria's role in the operation. Just as ECOWAS arose from a sustained Nigerian diplomatic initiative in the 1970s, ECOMOG depended heavily upon Nigerian policy and resources."

As in the case of the AU, the emergence of ECOWAS raises an interesting theoretical question. Do major paradigms, notably liberalism, constructivism and realism, account for the emergence of ECOWAS? Such a question is critically important with respect to the conditions under which ECOWAS emerged. How was it possible for other African leaders to follow Gnassingbé Eyadéma and Yakubu Gowon, both of whom took power through military coups? Most importantly, how was it possible for President Ibrahim Babangida of Nigeria to garner a consensus in order to spearhead the transformation of ECOWAS into a security community in the 1990s despite the persistent opposition and divergence of identities and values among the member states' leaders? It is important to note from the outset that since the three major paradigms have already been introduced in the preceding chapters, our discussion of these paradigms will focus less on reintroducing them than on analyzing their relevance with respect to the rise of ECOWAS.

II. The Liberal Paradigm

Does the liberal paradigm explain the emergence of ECOWAS? This will be the central question this section will attempt to address. To tackle this question, we will turn our attention to the conditions in which ECOWAS was born. But most importantly our attention will be focused on the conditions in which ECOWAS transformed from a primarily economic community to become a security community in 1990 with the creation of ECOMOG. As in the case of the African Union, the analysis of the usefulness of liberalism in explaining the rise of ECOWAS will be twofold. It will start by examining the liberal peace theory and it will then discuss the liberal analysis of Karl Deutsch.

The liberal peace argument is based on the idea that security communities emerge within the context of interactions between democracies. The rationale is explained very succinctly by Michael Howard (1978) who argues that democracies speak peace with each other because they share a "liberal conscience" (Howard 1978, 70). This assumption is built on the notion that states that form a security community share a collective identity of democratic values, which in turn constitutes a powerful inhibition tool against the belligerent dispositions of states. This position is largely derived from Kant's conceptualization of security communities based on a shared democratic ideal among the states of a given community. The contemporary proponents of this tradition frequently use the case of NATO to demonstrate that democratic security communities are cemented by liberal values (Williams 2001). The case of NATO, according to the liberal argument, is an illustration that the establishment of liberal institutions and norms is a sine qua non condition for peace.

The liberal argument regarding the emergence of security communities, however, is dominated by the contributions of Karl Deutsch. Deutsch's conceptualization of security communities has been widely discussed in the previous chapter. The purpose of this section of this chapter is to discuss the usefulness of Deutsch's theory with respect to the case of ECOWAS. In other words, does the emergence of ECOWAS take place in the manner in which Deutsch predicts? In order to address this question, it may be important to note briefly that for Deutsch (1954, 33) a security community is considered to be a group which has become integrated, where integration is defined as the attainment of a sense of community, accompanied by formal or informal institutions or practices, sufficiently strong and widespread to assure peaceful change among members of a group with 'reasonable' certainty over a 'long' period of time."

Most importantly, Deutsch et al. (1957) identify a series of fourteen conditions that are sine qua non for the rise of security communities. Among such conditions, he identifies three that are most essential for the emergence of both types of security communities. The first one is shared values and expectations. The second one is capabilities and communication processes. And the third one is mutual predictability of behavior. ECOWAS fits into the category of pluralistic security communities since the institutions of African states are not amalgamated. Instead the states that form this security community, as in the case of the African Union, have retained their sovereignties. To what extent do these three conditions fit the case of ECOWAS?

The merits of Deutsch's argument, when applied to the case of ECOWAS, are undeniable. Such merits lie first and foremost in Deutsch's recognition of the centrality of elites in the development of security communities. Like the AU, ECOWAS is clearly a product of Africa's leadership, as we have argued in the first section of this chapter. In addition, the strength of Deutsch's theory can be measured in terms of Deutsch's second condition. As a security community, ECOWAS, like the African Union, strengthens Deutsch's concept of capabilities and communication processes. Deutsch argues that the strength of such communication between the different political units that compose the community must be supported by some core states with markedly superior economic growth. ECOWAS is mainly supported by West Africa's economic giant: Nigeria.

However, the case of ECOWAS, just as in the case of the African Union, may constitute an insurmountable challenge for Deutsch and his collaborators in two of Deutsch's three major conditions. The first one is related to the concept of shared political and social values and expectations among the political elites. At this level it will suffice to point to the fact that ECOWAS emerged despite the fact that West Africa, in 1975 as well as in 1990, was clearly not a democratic zone for two essential reasons. First, only two states out of the original sixteen member states of ECOWAS were led by presidents who were democratically elected.[3] In addition, the transparency of such elections is the subject of a lot of questions.

Second, as Table I shows, the member states of ECOWAS, at the time of the rise of ECOWAS, did not perform well on some major democratic indicators such as political rights (PR) and civil liberties (CL). Table I is drawn from the country reports of Freedom House, a major international nongovernmental organization that conducts research and advocacy on democracy, political freedom and human rights. In their survey, political rights and civil liberties are measured on a one-to-seven scale, with one representing the highest degree of freedom and seven the lowest. Table I shows that, from 1972 when the first reports became available up to the rise of ECOWAS in 1975, only one member state of ECOWAS (the Gambia) out of its sixteen member states had acceptable scores with respect to political rights and civil liberties. Even worse, most West African states frequently reached the lowest possible scores.

Second, it is important to note that, for two essential reasons, the scores on political rights and civil liberties did not improve much with ECOWAS' mutation from a primarily economic community into a security community in 1990 with the emergence of ECOMOG. First, this period has seen only four

---

3 By 1975, only Leopold S. Senghor of Senegal and Siaka Stevens of Sierra Leone were elected as presidents of their respective countries. Yet, they managed to govern without regard to some basic political rights and civil liberties. All fourteen others became president without regular elections. Source: African Elections Database, available at http://africanelections.tripod.com, (accessed December 22, 2008.

Table 1: Political Rights (PR) and Civil Liberties (CL) in all ECOWAS member states up to the emergence of ECOWAS in 1975

YEARS COVERED	1972		1973		1974		1975	
	PR	CL	PR	CL	PR	CL	PR	CL
Benin	7	5	7	5	7	6	7	7
Burkina Faso	3	4	3	4	6	4	6	4
Cape Verde	NA	NA	NA	NA	NA	NA	5	5
Côte D'Ivoire	6	6	6	6	6	6	6	5
The Gambia	2	2	2	2	2	2	2	2
Ghana	6	6	7	6	7	5	7	5
Guinea	7	7	7	7	7	7	7	7
Guinea Bissau	NA	NA	NA	NA	6	6	6	6
Liberia	6	6	6	5	6	3	6	4
Mali	7	6	7	6	7	6	7	7
Mauritania	6	6	6	6	5	6	6	6
Niger	6	6	6	6	5	6	6	6
Nigeria	6	4	6	4	6	4	6	5
Senegal	6	6	6	6	6	5	6	4
Sierra Leone	4	5	6	5	6	5	6	5
Togo	7	5	7	5	7	6	7	6

Source: Freedom House, available at www.freedomhouse.org, accessed December 22, 2008.

elected presidents who participated in multiparty elections.[4] The transparency of those elections, however, like the transparency of the election in the first case, is subject to a lot of questions. Second and, most importantly, as Table II shows, the scores of ECOWAS's member states from 1987 up to the emergence of ECOMOG in 1990 remain dismal at best with respect to political rights and civil liberties. As in the case of the scores of 1975, the scores of ECOWAS and ECOMOG member countries between 1987 and 1990 frequently reached the lowest possible levels. This, in itself, constitutes one of the biggest challenges to the liberal paradigm in the sense that it shows that ECOWAS emerged as a community in general in 1975 and as a security community in particular in 1990, despite the fact that its member states did not share in the democratic principles of governance.

With respect to the third condition, mutual predictability of behavior, the emergence of ECOWAS, just like the rise of the African Union, illustrates the limits of Deutsch's liberal theory in accounting for security communities in Africa. It is important to recall that at the heart of Deutsch's theory, as illustrated by his Scandinavian example, rests the idea that the absence of a history

---

4   These four elections involved Houphouët-Boigny of Côte D'Ivoire, Dawda K. Jawara of the Gambia, Abou Diouf of Senegal and Joseph Momoh of Sierra Leone. Source: African Elections Database, available at http://africanelections.tripod.com, accessed December 21, 2008.

Table 2: Political Rights (PR) and Civil Liberties (CL) in all ECOWAS member states up to the emergence of ECOMOG in 1990

YEARS COVERED	1987		1988		1989		1990	
	PR	CL	PR	CL	PR	CL	PR	CL
Benin	7	7	7	7	7	7	6	4
Burkina Faso	7	6	7	6	6	5	6	5
Cape Verde	5	6	5	6	6	5	5	5
Côte D'Ivoire	6	5	6	6	6	5	6	4
The Gambia	3	3	3	3	2	2	2	2
Ghana	7	6	6	6	6	5	6	5
Guinea	7	6	7	6	7	6	6	5
Guinea Bissau	6	7	6	7	6	6	6	5
Liberia	5	5	5	5	6	5	7	7
Mali	7	6	6	6	6	6	6	5
Mauritania	6	6	6	6	7	6	7	6
Niger	7	6	6	6	7	6	6	5
Nigeria	6	5	5	5	6	5	5	5
Senegal	3	4	3	4	4	3	4	3
Sierra Leone	5	5	5	5	6	5	6	5
Togo	6	6	6	6	6	6	6	6

Source: Freedom House, available at www.freedomhouse.org, accessed December 22, 2008.

of aggressive behavior from one state to another makes it a safe bet to assume that the invasion of one country by another is highly improbable.

Yet, a cursory look at the recent history of West Africa reveals that such a bet could not safely be made. Examples of aggressive behaviors between dyads of West African countries are not hard to come by. The Mano River Wars are a good case in point. Since the 1990s, sustained and armed conflict in the Mano River basin has spread across the borders of at least four West African states, including Liberia, Sierra Leone, Ivory Coast and Guinea, and has engulfed the region in a severe humanitarian crisis.[5] The intervention of Senegal into its neighbor the Gambia in 1981 in an attempt to save the endangered regime of Dawda Diawara constitutes yet another example of countries living side by side but not in peace. Nevertheless, ECOWAS and particularly ECOMOG emerged as a security community despite such a history of aggressive behavior.

Moreover, as in the case of Africa in general, two problems could, at the very least, stem from explaining the West African experience in light of the Deutschian paradigm. The first is that although interstate wars are becoming a rarity in West Africa, a different type of war has persisted despite the emergence of the ECOWAS and ECOMOG. In this respect, civil wars which pullulate

---

5 Global Security, available at http://www.globalsecurity.org/military/world/war/mano-river. html,accessed December 22, 2008.

in the West African region, such as the ones in Ivory Coast and Sierra Leone, could not be satisfactorily accounted for by Deutsch. The second problem is related to the leadership variable. Although Deutsch's theory recognizes the centrality of leadership in the development of security communities, it tends to subordinate the impact of leadership to his three conditions. And as we have just argued, two of those three conditions are violated in the African case.

In sum, as a major paradigm of international integration, liberalism does not satisfactorily explain the emergence of security communities in West Africa. The evidence, as we have shown, lies in the fact that liberalism failed to predict the emergence of ECOWAS as a general community in 1975 and it fails to explain the mutation of ECOWAS from a general economic and political community into a security community.

III. The Constructivist Paradigm

Does the constructivist paradigm explain the emergence of ECOWAS? This is one of the central questions which the constructivist paradigm must address. As in the preceding section, our analysis will first take into account the main tenets of constructivism as they relate to the rise of security communities. Second, we will turn our attention toward the conditions in which ECOWAS emerged. Third, and most importantly, our attention will be focused on the condition in which ECOWAS moved from a primarily economic community to become a security community in 1990 with the creation of ECOMOG.

It may be worthwhile to reiterate at the outset that the constructivist paradigm is structured around the notion that communities in general and security communities in particular emerge out of shared identity between the member states of a given community. In this respect, the emergence of a security community can be understood in terms of changes in ideas, norms and processes. Alexander Wendt (1992) explains that the emergence of social structures is a function of some shared understandings, expectations or knowledge within a given community. As we argued in the previous chapter, the transatlantic community is widely seen by constructivists as a major case in point where a community of identity is the primary basis for the emergence of a security community (Jepperson, Wendt and Katzenstein 1996, 62). For Jepperson, Wendt and Katzenstein, this community between Israel and Western democracies, in spite of the fact that Israel shares contiguous borders with her Arab neighbors, is a clear indication that identity trumps geography in the formation of security communities. Constructivists also point to the fact that, as a security community, the transatlantic community is mainly made of Western European states and the United States instead of between the latter and the Soviet Union as yet another case for their argument (Risse-Kappen 1996).

It is also worthwhile to take into account John Ruggie's (1998) contributions, which are built around three core arguments. First, for Ruggie, the existence of core states is a sine qua non for the emergence of a security community. He uses the examples of Prussia in the process of German unification in the nineteenth century; Piedmont in Italy; Sweden in the pluralistic Scandinavian community and the United States in the transatlantic organization to make his case. In the case of ECOWAS, Nigeria fulfills that condition. Second, using the case of NATO, he contends that security communities follow and complement the economic and cultural ties of the member states (Ruggie 1998, 231).

In other words, for Ruggie, in order to understand why security communities emerge, we must take into account the broader dynamics of economic, political and cultural settings. For him, such economic integration constitutes the necessary condition, and the security mechanism is the sufficient condition for integration. Finally, while acknowledging the inherent difficulties that are associated with determining the exact causal mechanisms that lead to the emergence of a security community, he suggests that external threats from the Soviet Union, in the case of NATO, may be the single most decisive factor. Nevertheless, other factors such as economic integration, common bonds in civil society, market economy and constitutional democracy have also played their part. In sum, Ruggie's argument, like those of his constructivist predecessors, is built around the argument that the emergence of security communities is a function of shared identities and internalized beliefs.[6]

Finally, it is also important to reiterate that the constructivist explanation of the emergence of security communities is highly reconcilable with the liberal explanation. As an example, Thomas Risse-Kappen's analysis, which we referred to in the preceding chapter, could be quite informative. Although his analysis is centered on the democratic peace argument, he offers a constructivist variety of the same essential liberal argument. For him, pluralistic security communities are more likely to emerge out of democracies because democracies tend to perceive in each other a predisposition for peace. This shared collective identity is what makes democracies particularly predisposed to form international institutions that are aimed at consolidating the peace among democracies (Risse-Kappen 1995, 37). Emmanuel Adler and Michael Barnett's argument constitutes another illustration of the grey area that separates the two traditions of constructivism and liberalism in their accounts of the emergence of security communities.

They contend that the formation of communities is a result of the interactions between actors sharing common values, norms and symbols that provide a social identity. For them, such interactions reflect long-term interest, diffuse reciprocity and trust. Thus, for the authors, communities exist at the international level and security politics is profoundly shaped by such communities. Furthermore, they maintain that "those states dwelling within an international community might develop a pacific disposition" toward each other (Adler and Barnett 1998, 1). In other words, there is a reinforcing effect between the twin concepts of security and community. Nicholas Onuf's discussion of security regimes (1989, 150) reinforces this notion. His contention that the formalization of international rules both within and among states could develop a peaceful predisposition between the different states that eventually form a security community could be understood in such light. To what extent does the constructivist paradigm account for the emergence of ECOWAS? This question will be analyzed in the last section of this chapter.

---

6 A more elaborate discussion of this point can be found in Chapter 4.

At this stage, it will suffice to point out that the rise of ECOWAS as a general community and its mutation from a general community into a security community with the creation of ECOMOG raises a host of difficult questions for the constructivist paradigm. How did the community emerge despite a lack of shared identities? Why did, for instance, other African leaders follow Gnassingbé Eyadéma and Yakubu Gowon, both of whom took power through military coups? Most importantly, how was it possible for President Ibrahim Babangida of Nigeria, who almost single-handedly spearheaded the transformation of ECOWAS into a security community in 1990. to garner a consensus despite the persistent opposition and divergence of identities and values among the member states leaders?[7]

IV. The Realist Paradigm

Examining the realist paradigm in relation to the emergence of security communities is both challenging and rewarding. It is challenging in the sense that realism does not deal directly with the concept of security community. As we argued in the previous chapter, among all three paradigms of international relations under review, realism is the theory that seems to deal the least with the question of security communities. In fact, as we argued in the discussion of the African Union, there is no explicit realist theory of security communities, and the notion of "security community" is not of common usage among political realists. As a matter of example, as we explained in the fourth chapter, neither the works of Morgenthau nor those of Waltz, two major realist thinkers, make an explicit mention of the concept of security community.

Nevertheless, as in the preceding chapters, a study of the usefulness of realism could be rewarding for a variety of reasons that may be worth reiterating. The most obvious reason may rest with the fact that the question of security itself is a key concept in the realist paradigm, both among the classical realists as well as among the structural realists. In addition, realists agree with constructivists and liberals that institutions do operate at the international level. They also share the idea, and this is especially true with regards to Deutsch, that such institutions are usually sustained by the most powerful states within the community. However, one of the major divides between realism on one hand and liberalism and constructivism on the other hand lies in their perceptions of the causal mechanisms that lead to the emergence of security communities. Whereas liberals and constructivists argue that institutional arrangements such as security communities arise out of shared identities and values, realists claim that such institutions emerge out of the desire of the most powerful states to maintain or even increase their share of power.

Mearsheimer, for instance, a leading structural realist, argues against the idea that the security of Europe during the Cold War was the result of the emergence of NATO. Instead, he contends that the real cause of Europe's peace

---

7   Most Francophone West African states, especially Burkina Faso and Côte D'Ivoire, opposed President Ibrahim Babangida's move to create ECOMOG.

and stability during the Cold War was the bipolar distribution of power in Europe. For him, NATO is only an intervening variable in this relationship (Mearsheimer 1994/1995, 14). In the same vein, realists argue that to the extent that such individual states need alliances to overcome the security dilemma, such alliances are only temporary and would disappear when the threats, which made them necessary, disappear (Waltz 1979, Mearsheimer 1990).

Thus, no serious study of security communities could exist without considering realist theories for at least two essential reasons. The first one is related to realism's focus on the crucial issues of war and peace. The realist idea of security alliances, which are created to overcome the security dilemma, constitutes too important a contribution in the debate to be ignored. In this vein, Robert Jervis's analysis of the conditions that lead to the creation of alliances constitutes a valuable starting point. He argues that cooperation is more likely when the gains from mutual cooperation and the costs of noncooperation are high. In addition, he contends, like Waltz, that the influence of geography is crucial to the creation of security alliances (Jervis 1978). The conditions in which ECOWAS emerged, which will be discussed in greater length in relation to these realist tenets in the next section, seem to lend some credibility to Jervis's argument.

The second and most important reason may be related to the nature of the particular security community under review in this chapter. In this respect, taking into account the fact that the other two major paradigms of security communities—namely, liberalism and constructivism—are faced with some difficult questions, an exploration of the realist paradigm may contribute significantly to the scholarship. This is all the more legitimate since the case of ECOWAS seems to obey some essential realist tenets. According Robert Keohane (1986, 7), realism contains three key assumptions. The first assumption is that realists take the state as their unit of analysis. The second assumption is that states seek power either as an end in itself or as a means to other ends. The final assumption is that overall states behave in rational ways. Most importantly for the purpose of this study, we should note that realist thinkers share the view that in a system in which the major purpose of sovereign states is survival and the maximization of power, states often resort to power politics (Thucydides 431 BC; Hobbes 1651; Morgenthau 1948). How useful is realism in accounting for the emergence of ECOWAS? This question will be examined in the next section.

V. The Emergence of ECOWAS and the Limits of the Paradigms of International Politics

The preceding sections have attempted to introduce three major paradigms that address the rise of security communities. This section seeks to weigh the merits and faults of these three paradigms in relation to the emergence of ECOWAS. Each of these three paradigms has strengths as well as weaknesses in explaining the emergence of ECOWAS and ECOMOG. The conditions in which ECOWAS and ECOMOG emerged, however, seem to give realism an edge. Although the liberal and constructivist accounts are useful in explaining the emergence of

ECOWAS as a security community, their accounts are faced with two major difficulties when applied to the West African case.

The first major problem is related to the processes that lead to the emergence of security communities. On this account, the constructivist paradigm's focus on process over structure constitutes a major problem in the case of ECOWAS. Although both the constructivists and the neorealists agree on the basic notion that anarchy explains the emergence of security communities or security alliances, they disagree on the mechanisms and processes that lead to their emergence. Whereas the constructivists argue that the emergence of a security community is determined less by the structure of the system than by identity and process, the realists argue the opposite. A careful analysis of the conditions under which ECOWAS and ECOMOG were created, however, reveals that the critical element may rest less in the process which led to community formation than in the structure of the community. In other words, although the emergence of ECOWAS as a security community is an obvious result of a "process," there is no evidence to suggest that process in this case holds a greater sway than structure.

The fact that the two major initial proponents of ECOWAS are President Gowon of Nigeria and President Eyadéma of Togo—who can be identified respectively with the Anglophone camp of West Africa and the Francophone camp of West Africa—may constitute one of the clearest signs that ECOWAS may have been based on a community of interest rather than on a community of identity. Although the functioning of ECOWAS may have been hindered by the division over the Anglophone and Francophone identity, its creation was not. As in the case of the African Union, the contiguous nature of the borders of this community is the decisive factor in the emergence of ECOWAS.

In other words, the geographical structure of the West African countries forming the security community seems to be more important than the process which created it—such a process may not have been possible in the absence of this existing structural reality. In this respect, ECOWAS, like the African Union, differs fundamentally from NATO or the European Union in the sense that membership is not necessarily determined by shared democratic principles and values. For this reason, the idea that identity trumps geostrategy (Jepperson, Wendt and Katzenstein 1996, 62) may be problematic in the African context. A security community in which all members belong to the same subregion shows all the inherent difficulties related to supporting such an argument.

The second major problem is related to the liberal/realist divide and can be located mainly in what each paradigm perceives to be essential to the rise of communities. While the liberals argue that shared democratic values are critically important, the realists point to power politics as the determinant variable. The emergence of ECOWAS amidst a lack of democratic values may constitute the biggest obstacle to the liberal paradigm and consequently the biggest asset for the realist argument. The reason for this rests mainly with the fact that the rise of ECOWAS and ECOMOG shows that structure could trump values (i.e., democratic values) in the emergence of security communities.

In addition, the explanatory power of the realist account is also manifest in the very institutional design of ECOWAS, which remains dominated by a web of interstate relationships. The dominance of the Authority of Heads of State and Government in decision making, the national representation in the Council of Ministers and the intergovernmental technical committees, the limited resources and responsibilities of the secretariats as well as the limited jurisdiction of the regional courts constitute some of the strongest indications of the centrality of the state system in the creation as well as in the functioning of the regional organization.[8]

This fact does not, however, signify that political realism provides a satisfactory explanation for the emergence of ECOWAS. Realism's focus on the state and power politics as an explanatory variable faces its own limits. Realism's focus on the state as the unit of analysis tends to oversimplify a very complex reality. In fact, through its focus on the state, the realist paradigm fails to account for a key variable, individual political leadership, which, as the rise of ECOWAS and ECOMOG shows, does play an essential role in the emergence of security communities.

As Walter Mattli (1999, 7) argues, many analysts have discarded the role of charismatic leaders as explanatory factors for integration. Their rationale for discarding individual leaders is based on their inability to explain the numerous failures of these leaders and the long phases of stagnation in the process of building international communities. For Mattli, the main problem with this explanation is not that it is wrong but that is insufficient. Such explanation may be insufficient because it underanalyzes the key role of individual leaders in the rise of security communities. The African experience, as exemplified by the case of ECOWAS in which individual political leaders played the central role in the rise of a community, questions these perceived notions both in terms of the outcomes of their actions as well as in terms of their motivations.

Nigerian President Ibrahim Babangida's use of the Standing Mediation Committee (SMC) of ECOWAS, for instance, to launch an intervention in Liberia's civil war had far-reaching motivations which go beyond interest and power alone. Babangida, himself would express such motivations both in moral and political terms. In an interview with the weekly West Africa he argued that Lagos "believe[d] that it would have been morally reprehensible and politically indefensible to stand by and watch while citizens of [Liberia] decimate[d] themselves" (Conteh-Morgan 1993, 37). However, as Mortimer notes, although there is no reason to question Babangida's moral claims, there is reason to place Babangida's actions into context. President Samuel Doe, whose regime was under siege, was a personal friend of President Babangida and had seen to it that the University of Liberia bestowed an honorary degree upon the Nigerian leader. Babangida, in turn, donated for the building of the School of International Affairs in Liberia (Mortimer 1996, 151).

This argument is supported by Deng and Zartman (2002, 19) who contend that President Ibrahim Babangida of Nigeria, a personal friend of Doe, sent ECOMOG to rescue Liberia and end a war that was launched from Ivory Coast and supported by Burkina Faso and, more distantly, Libya. These arguments

---

8   See the institutions of ECOWAS, available online at the official website of ECOWAS at http://www.sec.ecowas.int/index.html, accessed December 22, 2008.

point to the fact that the formation of communities does not only obey the logic of the state as an impersonal actor, it could also obey the logic of interpersonal relationships, which transcend and sometimes go against state interests and preferences. Nigeria became the main architect of the integration of West Africa despite its lukewarm attitude toward Pan-Africanism and integration (Nye 1965, 244) mainly because of the personal leadership of Ibrahim Babangida. Thus, the rise of ECOWAS and ECOMOG could also be understood in terms of the will of particular individual political leaders.

VI. Conclusion

This chapter has sought to test three major paradigms of international integration with respect to the West African experience. The institutional evolution of ECOWAS is much different from that of the African Union—contrary to the case of the AU, ECOWAS emerged primarily as a general political and economic community and mutated into a security community in 1990 with the creation of ECOMOG. Like the case of the African Union, the case of ECOWAS shows that the traditional paradigms of international politics do not fully explain the emergence of security communities in Africa. Also, like the case of the African Union, realism seems to provide a better explanation for the emergence of ECOWAS than liberalism and constructivism. For example, ECOWAS and ECOMOG show that security communities may also emanate partly from realpolitik.

The liberal argument, which is structured around the idea that security communities emerge out of shared democratic values, has shown its limits in the face of a community in which the vast majority of its members do not share in the democratic principle. The constructivist argument, which is built around the idea that security communities emerge out of shared identities, has also shown its limits in the face of a community created on the basis of shared borders. The realist paradigm seems to be more in sync with the conditions under which ECOWAS and ECOMOG emerged. Such conditions are based on a structural community rather than on a community of values and identity. Realism, however, falls short in its focus on the state as the unit of analysis. In light of all these facts, the case of ECOWAS, especially when the conditions of its birth as a general community and as a security community are taken into account, calls for a new set of hypotheses that will take into consideration a new set of variables that have been left on the margins of the scientific enquiries of the three major traditional paradigms.

Chapter 6

The Emergence of The SADC and The Limits of The Paradigms of International Politics

This chapter attempts to replicate the analysis made in Chapters 4 and 5 by using the case of the Southern African Development Community (SADC) in lieu of the AU and ECOWAS. In this sense, as in the two preceding chapters, the central question this chapter seeks to tackle is the following: Do liberalism, constructivism and realism explain the emergence of the SADC as a general community and as a security community? Headquartered in Gaborone, Botswana, the SADC is a community of fourteen southern African states.[1] The SADC was originally created on April 1, 1980, as the Southern African Development Coordination Conference (SADCC) and was transformed into the Southern African Development Community (SADC) on August 17, 1992.

The aims of the SADC are twofold: socioeconomic and political on one hand and security on the other. According to Oosthuizen (2006, 39), the aims of the SADC include (1) the promotion of economic growth and socioeconomic development and (2) the promotion and maintenance of peace, security and democracy through regional cooperation and integration. In this chapter, our main interest lies in the security aspect. In other words, does

---

1   The member states of SADC include Angola, Botswana, Lesotho, Malawi, Mozambique, Swaziland, Tanzania, Zambia, Zimbabwe, the Democratic Republic of the Congo, Mauritius, Namibia, Seychelles and South Africa. Seychelles had also previously been a member of SADC from 1997 to 2004.

the emergence of the SADC as a security community unfold in the ways in which the three major paradigms of international politics predict?

I. The SADC: Genesis of the Emergence of a Security Community

The institutional evolution of the SADC bears significant similarities as well as differences with both that of the African Union and ECOWAS. Such similarities and differences are especially significant between the SADC and ECOWAS— like ECOWAS, the SADC was originally created to serve primarily as a general economic and political community. However, unlike ECOWAS (whose mutation from a general community into a security community was a function of one defining event, the civil war in Liberia), the SADC's transition was the product of a much longer and smoother chain of events.

Created as the Southern African Development Coordination Conference (SADCC) in 1980 by nine founding members, the forerunner of the SADC originally included Angola, Botswana, Lesotho, Malawi, Mozambique, Swaziland, Tanzania, Zambia and Zimbabwe. The SADCC was created mainly to guarantee the collective self-reliance of its member states. Most specifically, its primary goal was to create a framework for regional integration and at the same time reduce the economic and military dependence of the southern African region on the outside world in general and on Apartheid South Africa in particular (Deng and Zartman 2002, 50). Its original aims also included the coordination of political, diplomatic and military struggles against all remaining colonial and white minority regimes in the southern African region (Oosthuizen 2006, 40). These objectives are clearly summed in the charter of the SADC and they include "coordinating development projects in order to lessen economic dependence on the then apartheid South Africa."[2]

The Lusaka Declaration of April 1, 1980, amidst an anti-Apartheid climate, paved the way for the establishment of the SADCC in July 1981, as it constituted the framework from which the SADCC was built. The declaration was structured around four major economic objectives which included the reduction of economic dependence mainly vis-à-vis Apartheid South Africa; the creation of the mechanism for regional integration; the mobilization of regional resources to promote the implementation of national, interstate and regional policies and the establishment of concerted action in order to secure international cooperation (Oosthuizen 2006, 59). The roots of the SADCC and the SADC can be traced back to the 1970s when political leaders such as Julius Nyerere of Tanzania, Kenneth Kaunda of Zambia and Seretse Khama of Botswana, yearning for freedom from colonial and white minority rule, spurred the creation of the loose and informal grouping known as the Front Line States (FLS) (Oosthuizen 2006, 53; Schoeman 2002, 3).

It is also important to note that the SADCC did not take on any security functions. Such security responsibility was taken on by the informal FLS, a

---

2   Available at the SADC's official website at http://www.sadc.int, accessed December 22, 2008.

network made of individual heads of state who knew each other personally and who arrived at agreements with little recourse to the niceties of diplomacy or bureaucratic process (Cawthra 1997). In particular, two individual leaders played a key role in the establishment and functioning of the FLS. The first was Julius Nyerere of Tanzania and the second was Kenneth Kaunda of Zambia. The informal structures, which were built with the creation of the FLS, would constitute the framework on which future leaders such as Robert Mugabe of Zimbabwe would later base the establishment of the SADCC in 1980 (Cawthra 1997, 3).

The early 1990s, which coincided with the near end of the Apartheid system in South Africa, constitute one of the most decisive periods in the institutional evolution of the integration framework in southern Africa. As the southern African region began to face new challenges by the early 1990s, a transformation of the SADCC into a new and more formal and more structured type of regional organization was needed. Such challenges went beyond the traditional development, economic and trade challenges to include security challenges. As we argued in Chapter 3 in our discussion of Africa's communities, most of the challenges threatening the security of the citizens of the subregion and their goods could not be faced by any one single state; they called for a collective and coordinated response. Thus, the Windhoek declaration and treaty of August 17, 1992, which consecrated the transformation of the SADCC into the SADC, could be understood in the context of the realization by member states of southern Africa that economic development, which is associated with the free movement of people and their goods, could not take place amidst a security vacuum. The creation in August 1995 of the Southern African Regional Police Chiefs Cooperation Organization (SARPCCO), an organ specifically designed to reduce cross-border crime, is a clear additional indication of the SADC's commitment to a secure southern Africa (Deng and Zartman 2002, 52). Such a security mechanism needed to go beyond the informal structures of the FLS and the SADCC in order to be included in the more formal framework of a re-modeled southern African community. Thus, the beginning of the 1990s marks the first genuine emergence of a security community in southern Africa amidst a divided and war-torn subregion (Cilliers 1999).

The new goals of the SADC include mainly the development and economic growth of the region and the promotion of peace and security in southern Africa. This chapter will focus on the second aspect of the SADC: the security aspect. As we argued in Chapter 3, the clearest articulation of the security component of the SADC resides in the institution of the Organ on Politics, Defense and Security (OPDS) (Ngoma 2005, 183). As one of the main organs of the SADC, the OPDS's main purpose is to guarantee collective security by identifying common threats. In addition, the OPDS is committed to resolving potential security challenges in the southern African region (Ngoma 2005, 146). In the words of Oosthuizen, the objectives of the OPDS include the peaceful prevention, containing and resolving of inter- and intra-state conflict, including the use of military enforcement if necessary. As such, the OPDS has some-times been referred to mischievously as Mugabe's Organ because of President Mugabe's role in its creation. According to Oosthuizen (2006, 213), the OPDS constitutes the SADC's most important structure that has been associated with the promotion of peace and security in southern Africa.

In sum, the move from the SADCC in 1980 to the SADC in 1992 marks the birth of a security community. Article 5 of the SADC charter is quite clear with respect to its aims: "The region needs, therefore, to establish a framework and mechanisms to strengthen regional solidarity; and provide for mutual peace and security" (Deng and Zartman 2002, 51). According to Gina Schalkwyk of the Institute for Security Studies, the SADC regards itself effectively as a security community (Schalkwyk 2005, 21). Today, the SADC consists of fourteen states after the Democratic Republic of the Congo, Madagascar, Mauritius, Namibia, Seychelles and South Africa joined the original nine member states of the SADCC.

The role of the political leadership of southern Africa in the emergence of the SADC, as in the emergence of its forerunners, can never be stressed enough. In fact, "the formation of SADC was the culmination of a long process of consultations by the leaders of southern Africa."[3] The role of these leaders range from the contributions of Nyerere and Kaunda in the creation of the FLS and the SADCC to the contributions of Robert Mugabe of Zimbabwe both in the formation of the SADCC as well as in the transformation of the SADCC into the SADC.

The expectations of the SADC are clearly laid out in the SADC official website and they include

- sovereign equality of all member states;
- solidarity, peace and security;
- human rights, democracy and the rule of law;
- equity, balance and mutual benefit and
- peaceful settlement of disputes.

Like the African Union and ECOWAS, the SADC fits into Deutsch's concept of a pluralistic security community. In addition, as in the case of the AU and ECOWAS, the emergence of the SADC raises an interesting theoretical question. Do major paradigms of international integration—notably, liberalism, constructivism and realism—account for the emergence of the SADC? Before addressing this crucial question, it is important to note, as we did in the preceding chapter, that since the three major paradigms have already been introduced in previous chapters, our discussion of these paradigms will focus less on reintroducing them than on analyzing their relevance with respect to the SADC.

II. The Liberal Paradigm

Does the liberal paradigm explain the emergence of the SADC? This will be the central question of this section. As in the case of ECOWAS, we will consider the conditions in which the SADCC was born in 1980, and most importantly, this section will focus on the condition in which the SADCC was transformed

---

3   See the website of SADC available at http://www.sadc.int, accessed December 21, 2008.

into a security community in 1992 when it became the SADC. As in the case of the African Union and ECOWAS, our analysis of the usefulness of liberalism in explaining the rise of the SADC will be twofold. It will start first by examining briefly the arguments of the liberal peace theory and second it will move the focus to Karl Deutsch's seminal argument.

The liberal peace argument is structured around the idea that security communities emerge within the context of interactions between democracies. According to Michael Howard (1978, 70) the peace among democracies is based on a shared "liberal conscience." The position of the liberal peace argument is largely derived from Kant's conceptualization of security communities based on a shared democratic ideal among the states of a given community. The contemporary proponents of this tradition frequently use the case of the transatlantic organization to demonstrate that democratic security communities are cemented by liberal values (Williams 2001). The case of NATO, according to the liberal argument, is an illustration that the establishment of liberal institutions and norms is a sine qua non condition for peace.

The liberal argument regarding the emergence of security communities, however, remains dominated by the contributions of Karl Deutsch. Deutsch's conceptualization of security communities has been widely discussed in the previous chapters. The purpose of this section is to discuss the usefulness of Deutsch's theory with respect to the case of the SADC. In other words, does the emergence of the SADC take place in the manners in which Deutsch's liberal theory predicts? Specifically does the emergence of the SADC fit into Deutsch's three major conditions for the rise of security communities?

It may be worthwhile to reiterate that Deutsch's first condition is shared values and expectations. His second condition is capabilities and communication processes that are supported by core states with markedly superior economies. And his third condition is mutual predictability of behavior. The SADC, like the AU and ECOWAS, is in line with Deutsch's conceptualization of pluralistic security communities in the sense that the institutions of the states of southern Africa are not amalgamated. Instead the states that form the southern African security community have retained their sovereignties. Like the case of the AU and ECOWAS, the case of the SADC raises one important question: To what extent do Deutsch's three conditions fit the case of the SADC?

The merits of Deutsch's argument, when applied to the case of the SADCC and the SADC, are undeniable. As in the case of the AU and ECOWAS, such merits lie mainly in the author's recognition of the centrality of elites in the development of security communities. The SADC is no exception to Deutsch's rule. The importance of southern Africa's leaders in the creation of the SADC has been suggested in the preceding section.

However, contrary to the cases of the AU and ECOWAS, which revealed the strength of Deutsch's second condition, the integration experiment in southern Africa lends Deutsch's argument an explanatory power that is mixed at best. Specifically, the SADCC, the forerunner of the SADC, highlights the limits of Deutsch's concept of capabilities and communication processes. For Deutsch, the strength of such communication processes between the different political units that compose the community must be supported by some core states with markedly superior economic growth. The case of the SADCC, which emerged precisely in order to rid southern Africa of its economic and military dependence on the most powerful economy of the subregion(South Africa), may constitute a non-negligible obstacle to Deutsch's second condition.

Contrary to ECOWAS, whose creation is mainly driven by Nigeria (West Africa's economic giant), the SADCC emerged in spite of South Africa (the most meaningful economic and military force of the region). Furthermore, the SADCC emerged as a bulwark against South Africa in spite of the fact that successive South African leaders—notably Jan Smuts, Hendrik Verwoerd and Peter Botha—relentlessly promoted the notion of economic, political and security community in southern Africa on the basis of South African leadership (Cawthra 1997, 3). However, the emergence of the SADC in 1992 could be seen as more compatible with Deutsch's second—as the largest economy and military power up to the emergence of the SADC, Zimbabwe, under Mugabe, played the most crucial role in the emergence and functioning of the subcontinental bloc.

This is particularly true of the ways in which Zimbabwe's transition to black majority rule in 1980 (with the rise of Mugabe to power) made it possible for the SADCC to operate as an effective anti-Apartheid bloc (Sidaway and Gibb 1998, 169). In addition, this period coincided with the near end of the Apartheid system, with South Africa starting to claim its role as the leader of the southern African region. With military spending that outweighs the rest of the SADC countries combined (Cawthra 1997, 25), South Africa's dominance in the southern African community is indisputable.

Furthermore, the case of the SADC, just like the cases of African Union and ECOWAS, may constitute an insurmountable challenge for Deutsch and his collaborators' arguments in their two other major conditions. The first one is related to the concept of shared political and social values and expectations among the political elites. At this level, like in the case of the AU and ECOWAS, it will suffice to point to the fact that the SADCC emerged in 1980 and the SADC in 1992, in spite the fact that southern Africa was clearly not a democratic subregion for these two periods. The evidence for this lies first in the fact that only two states out the original nine member states of the SADCC were led by presidents who were democratically elected.[4] Second, as Table III shows, southern African states, at the time of the rise of the SADC, did not perform well on some major democratic indicators such as political rights (PR) and civil liberties (CL). Table III is drawn from the country reports of Freedom House, a major international nongovernmental organization that conducts research and advocacy on democracy, political freedom and human rights. In their survey, political rights and civil liberties are measured on a one-to-seven scale, with one representing the highest degree of freedom and seven the lowest. Table III shows that, from 1977 up to the rise of the SADC in 1980, only one out of the nine member states of the SADC (Botswana) had acceptable scores with respect to political rights and civil liberties. Worse yet, most southern African states frequently reached the lowest possible scores.

---

4 By 1980, only Botswana and Lesotho held regular elections. Source: African Elections Database, available at http://africanelections.tripod.com, accessed December 21, 2008.

Table 3: Political Rights (PR) and Civil Liberties (CL) in all the SADCC member states up to the emergence of the SADC in 1980

YEARS COVERED	1977		1978		1979		1980	
	PR	CL	PR	CL	PR	CL	PR	CL
Angola	7	7	7	7	7	7	7	7
Botswana	2	3	2	3	2	2	2	3
Lesotho	5	4	5	5	5	5	5	5
Malawi	7	6	6	7	6	7	6	7
Mozambique	7	7	7	7	7	7	7	7
Swaziland	6	5	6	5	5	5	5	5
Tanzania	6	6	6	6	6	6	6	6
Zambia	5	5	5	5	5	5	5	6
Zimbabwe	6	5	5	5	4	4	3	4

Source: Freedom House, available at www.freedomhouse.org, accessed December 21, 2008.

Finally, it is important to note that, for two essential reasons, the scores on some major democratic indexes are, at best, mixed with the SADCC's mutation into a security community in 1992 with the. The first reason lies in the fact that although this period constitutes an improvement from 1980—in the sense that it has seen five out of the ten presidents of the SADC's member states elected[5] in somewhat regular elections—the fact remains that the community is far from being a democratic zone.[6]

The second reason is related to the performance of the SADC member states on political rights and civil liberties. As Table IV shows, the scores of the SADCC's member states from 1989 up to the emergence of the SADC in 1992 remain dismal at best with respect to political rights and civil liberties. It is important to note that Table IV takes into account only ten out of the fourteen current countries which make up the SADC. The reason is that only ten countries were member states of the SADC at the time of its birth. The rest of the member states joined at later stages.[7] As in the case of the scores of 1980, the scores of the SADC member countries between 1989 and 1992, with the exception of Botswana, frequently reached the lowest possible levels. This, in itself, constitutes one of the most significant challenges to the liberal paradigm; it shows that the SADC emerged as a security community 1992 despite the fact that its member states did not share in the democratic principles of governance.

---

5   The following member states which include Angola, Botswana, Lesotho, Zambia and Zimbabwe did hold regular elections in the period up to the creation of the SADC.

6   Source: African Elections Database, available at http://africanelections.tripod.com, accessed December 12, 2008.

7   South Africa joined on August 30, 1994; Mauritius joined on August 28, 1995; the Democratic Republic of the Congo joined on September 8, 1997, and Madagascar joined on August 18, 2005. As for Seychelles, it joined on September 8, 1997, and opted out on July 1, 2004.

Table 4: Political Rights (PR) and Civil Liberties (CL) in all the SADC member states up to the emergence of the SADC in 1992

YEARS COVERED	1989		1990		1991		1992	
	PR	CL	PR	CL	PR	CL	PR	CL
Angola	7	7	7	7	7	7	6	6
Botswana	1	2	1	2	1	2	1	2
Lesotho	6	5	6	5	6	4	6	4
Malawi	7	6	7	6	7	6	6	7
Mozambique	6	7	6	6	6	4	6	4
Swaziland	6	5	6	5	6	5	6	5
Tanzania	6	5	6	5	6	5	6	5
Zambia	6	5	6	5	2	3	2	3
Zimbabwe	6	4	6	4	5	4	5	4
Namibia	4	3	2	3	2	3	2	2

Source: Freedom House, available at www.freedomhouse.org, accessed December 21, 2008.

With respect to the third condition, mutual predictability of behavior, the emergence of the SADC, just like the rise of the African Union and ECOWAS, highlights the limits of Deutsch's liberal arguments in explaining the rise of security communities in Africa. At the heart of Deutsch's argument, as illustrated by his Scandinavian example, rests the idea that the absence of a history of aggressive behavior from one state to another makes it a safe bet for countries to assume that the invasion of one country by another is highly improbable. Yet, a cursory look at the recent history of southern Africa reveals that such an argument may not hold. South Africa's conflicting relationship with its neighbors up to the end of the Apartheid system in the beginning of the 1990s constitutes one of the most potent reminders that the condition of mutual predictability of peaceful behavior may not be met in the southern African subregion. In addition, the fact that the Democratic Republic of the Congo, a member state of the SADC, is the conflict theater of six contending states each involved on one side or another may constitute the most tragic illustration of the absence of a history of aggressive state behavior among the members of the SADC (Braeckman 1999; Tschiyembe 1999). Furthermore such aggressive behavior involves at least three SADC states, including Angola, Zimbabwe and Namibia.

Moreover, as in the case of Africa in general and West Africa in particular, two problems could at the very least stem from explaining the southern African experience in light of the Deutschian paradigm. The first is that although direct military confrontations between two states in southern Africa are becoming a thing of the past, a different type of war has persisted despite the emergence of the SADCC and the SADC. In this sense, the long-fought civil war in the Democratic Republic of the Congo, which we alluded to earlier, remains a puzzle which Deutsch's theory has yet to solve. The second problem is related to the leadership variable. Although Deutsch's theory recognizes the centrality of leadership in the development of security communities, it tends to subordinate the impact of leadership to his three conditions. And as we have shown both in the case of the AU and ECOWAS, two of those three conditions are violated. In the case of the SADC, two of those conditions are violated and the other one applies to the SADC only in a mixed fashion.

In sum, as a major paradigm of international integration, liberalism does not satisfactorily explain the emergence of a security community in southern Africa. The evidence, as we have shown, lies in the fact that liberalism fails to predict the emergence of the FLS and the SADCC as informal communities and fails to predict the SADC as a more institutionalized community in 1992. Although the SADC's August 2003/2004 admission criteria clearly stipulate that the applicant should be "well versed with and share the SADC's ideals and aspirations set out in the SADC treaty" (Oosthuizen 2006, 135), the reality remains very different. Such ideals and aspirations include the adherence to the principles of democracy, human rights and the rule of law and as the evidence shows otherwise.

III. The Constructivist Paradigm

Does the constructivist paradigm explain the emergence the SADC? As in the two previous chapters, this is one of the central questions that the constructivist paradigm must address. As in the preceding section, our analysis will first take into account the main tenets of constructivism as they relate to the rise of security communities. Second, our attention will be focused on the conditions in which the SADCC emerged as a general community as well as on the conditions in which the SADC evolved from the SADCC in 1992.

It is important to point out, at the outset, that the constructivist paradigm is structured around the notion that communities in general and security communities in particular emerge out of shared identity between the member states that form a given community. According to Alexander Wendt (1992), the emergence of social structures is a product of shared understandings, expectations or knowledge within a given community. Wendt and his constructivist colleagues usually point to the transatlantic community as a major example of a situation in which a community of identity is the primary basis for the emergence of a security community (Jepperson et al. 1996, 62). For Jepperson, Wendt and Katzenstein, NATO, a community between Israel and Western democracies in spite of the fact that Israel shares contiguous geographical borders with her Arab neighbors, is a clear indication that identity trumps geography in the formation of security communities. Constructivists also point to the fact that, as a security community, the transatlantic community is mainly made of Western European states and the United States (instead of the latter and the Soviet Union) as yet an additional case for their argument (Risse-Kappen 1996).

While analyzing the constructivist argument with respect to the emergence of security communities, it is also worthwhile to take into account John Ruggie's (1998) study which is built around three major arguments. First, for Ruggie, the existence of core states is a sine qua non for the emergence of a security community. He uses the examples of Prussia in the process of German unification in the nineteenth century, Piedmont in Italy, Sweden in the pluralistic Scandinavian community and the United States in the transatlantic organization to make his case. In the case of the SADC, Zimbabwe, the most dynamic economic unit in the community at the time of the emergence of the SADC and prior to the end of Apartheid in South Africa, fulfills that condition.

Second, Ruggie's use of the case of NATO to make the point that security communities follow and complement the economic and cultural ties of the member states (Ruggie 1998, 231) may be of great value for our understanding of the dynamics around the formation of security communities. In other words, in order to understand why security communities emerge, we must take into account the broader dynamics of economic, political and cultural settings. For Ruggie, such economic integration constitutes the necessary condition, and the security mechanism is the sufficient condition for integration. Finally, while acknowledging the inherent difficulties that are associated with determining the exact causal mechanisms that lead to the emergence of a security community, he suggests that, in the case of NATO, external threats from the Soviet Union may be the single most decisive factor. Nevertheless other factors such as economic integration, common bonds in civil society, market economy and constitutional democracy have also played their part. In sum, Ruggie's argument, like those of his constructivist predecessors, is built around the idea that the emergence of security communities is a function of a broad set of factors that are cemented by shared identities and internalized beliefs.

Finally, it is also important to reiterate that the constructivist explanation of the emergence of security communities is built around an argument that is highly reconcilable with the liberal argument. As an example, Thomas Risse-Kappen's analysis, which we referred to in the two preceding chapters, could be quite informative. Although his analysis is centered on the democratic peace argument, he offers a constructivist variety of the same liberal argument. For him, pluralistic security communities are more likely to emerge out of democracies because democracies tend to see each other as vectors of peace. This shared collective identity is what makes democracies particularly predisposed to form international institutions that are aimed at consolidating the peace among democracies (Risse-Kappen 1995, 37). Adler and Barnett's (1998) argument converges along similar lines and constitutes another illustration of the grey area separating the two traditions of constructivism and liberalism in their accounts of the emergence of security communities.

At the heart of their argument lies the notion that the creation of communities is a result of the interactions between actors sharing common values, norms and symbols that provide a social identity. For Adler and Barnett, such interactions reflect long-term interest, diffuse reciprocity and trust. Thus, for the authors, communities exist at the international level and security politics is profoundly shaped by them. Moreover, they maintain that "those states dwelling within an international community might develop a pacific disposition" toward each other (Adler and Barnett 1998, 1). In other words, there is a reinforcing effect between the twin concepts of security and community. Nicholas Onuf's discussion of security regimes (1989, 150) reinforces this idea. His contention that the formalization of international rules both within and among states could develop a peaceful predisposition between the different states that eventually form a security community could be understood in such light. To what extent does the constructivist paradigm account for the emergence of the SADC? This question will be analyzed in the last section of this chapter.

At this stage, it will suffice to point out that the rise of the SADCC and its mutation into the SADC, like the two previous cases of the AU and ECOWAS, raises a host of difficult questions for the constructivist paradigm. One of the most salient of such thorny questions is, how did the SADCC and the SADC emerge and function under the leadership of Robert Mugabe despite the lack of shared identity between him and key leaders in southern Africa? Most generally, how did the SADC emerge in the context of divided identities among the leadership in southern Africa?

IV. The Realist Paradigm

As in the two preceding chapters, examining the realist paradigm in relation to the emergence of security communities can be both something of a challenge as well as something of a reward. It could be challenging, as we stressed in the two preceding chapters, in the sense that realism does not deal directly with the concept of security community. Among all three paradigms of international relations under review, realism seems to deal the least with the question of security communities; there is no explicit realist theory of security communities and the notion of "security community" is not of common usage among political realists. This case is illustrated by no better example than the fact that there is no explicit reference to the notion of security community in the works of Morgenthau or Waltz, two major realist thinkers. This lack of explicit mention of the concept may be explained by realism's focus on the state and on power politics as the prime way of overcoming the security dilemma. John Mearsheimer's (1994/1995) contention, in his seminal study of the post–Cold War security arrangements in Europe, and that the rejection of power politics as an organizing concept, is both misguided and dangerous should be understood in such light. For him, the promise of what he regards as the three major institutionalist theories—liberalism, collective security and critical theories—about regional peace through the development of regional institutions is a false one mainly because there is a fundamental flaw in the causal logic of these theories.

Nevertheless, examining the explanatory power of realism vis-à-vis the emergence of the SADC could be rewarding for a variety of reasons. One such reason rests in the fact that the question of security itself is a key concept among major realists, including the classical realists and the structural realists. In addition, like liberals and constructivists, realists argue that institutions do operate at the international level. They also share the idea, and this is especially true with respect to Deutsch, that such institutions are usually sustained by the most powerful states within the community. However, on the crucial question of explaining the rise of security communities, a gulf separates the realist tradition on one hand and the liberal and constructivist traditions on the other hand. Whereas liberals and constructivists argue that institutional arrangements such as security communities arise out of shared identities and values, realists claim that such institutions emerge out of the desire of the most powerful states to maintain and increase their share of power.

This realist contention based on power and interest is articulated perhaps best by Robert Jervis. According to Jervis, states are more likely to cooperate and form alliances when the gains from mutual cooperation and the costs of noncooperation are high. Furthermore, he contends, like Waltz, that the influence of geography is crucial to the creation of security alliances (Jervis 1978). The conditions in which the SADC emerged, which will be discussed in greater length in the next section, seems to lend some credibility to Jervis's argument.

In addition, the nature of the particular security community under review in this chapter may contribute more than any other factor to the explanatory power of the realist paradigm in the sense that the case of the SADC seems to obey some essential realist assumptions. Realists of all persuasions (i.e., classic and structural) share the view that, in a system in which the major purpose of sovereign states is survival and the maximization of power, states often resort to power politics and create alliances for the purpose of escaping the security dilemma. How useful is realism in accounting for the emergence of the SADC? This question will be examined in the next section.

V. The Emergence of the SADC and the Limits of the Paradigms of International Politics

The preceding sections of this chapter, as in the case of the preceding chapters, have attempted to introduce three major paradigms of international integration that address the rise of security communities. This section seeks to weigh the strengths and weaknesses of each of these three paradigms in relation to the emergence of the SADC. As in the cases of the AU and ECOWAS, each of the three paradigms has strengths as well as weaknesses in explaining the emergence of the SADC. The conditions in which the SADC emerged, however, seem to accord realism more explanatory power than liberalism and constructivism. Although the liberal and constructivist accounts are useful in explaining the emergence of the SADC as a security community, their accounts are faced with a good number of major difficulties when applied to the southern African case.

First, with respect to the constructivist paradigm, the first major problem is related to the processes that led to the emergence of the SADC. Specifically, the constructivist paradigm's focus on process over structure constitutes one such major problem. The problem with the constructivist account becomes more salient when it is confronted with the realist, and specially the neorealist, account. Although both the constructivists and the neorealists agree on the basic notion that anarchy explains the emergence of security communities or security alliances, they disagree on the mechanisms and processes which lead to their emergence. Whereas the constructivists argue that the emergence of a security community is determined less by the structure of the system than by identity and process, the realists take the opposite view.

In the particular case of the SADC, the evidence, which reveals itself with a careful analysis of the conditions under which the SADC emerged, suggests that the critical element may rest less in the process than in the structure of the community. In other words, although the emergence of the SADC as a security community is obviously the result of a "process," there is no evidence to suggest that process in this case holds a greater sway than structure. Rather, a community in which geographical proximity is key to membership points unmistakably to the overriding importance of structure. Otherwise how could this community have emerged under the leadership of President Robert Mugabe in the midst of a lack of identity at the elite level in southern Africa? For this reason, the idea that identity trumps geostrategy (Jepperson et al. 1996, 62) may be problematic in the southern African context. A security community in which all members belong to the same subregion shows all the inherent difficulties that are related to the universalist claims of the constructivist tradition.

The second major problem rests with the liberal paradigm when it is compared with the realist paradigm. Such divide between the two paradigms rests essentially in what each paradigm perceives to be essential to the rise of communities. While the liberals argue that shared democratic values are critically important, the realists point to power politics as the determinant variable. The emergence of the SADCC and the SADC amidst a lack of democratic values, as shown in Tables I and II, may constitute the biggest obstacle to the liberal paradigm and consequently the biggest strength of the realist argument. The reason for this lies mainly in the fact that the rise of the SADCC and the SADC shows that structure trumps values (i.e., democratic values) in the emergence of security communities. In this respect, the case of the SADC, like the case of the African Union and ECOWAS, differs fundamentally from that of NATO or the European Union in the sense that membership is not necessarily determined by shared democratic principles and values. As President Masire of Botswana argued in his address to the SADCC summit in 1992, the SADC emerged primarily "out of a common awareness of common interest" (Sidaway and Gibb 1998, 164).

This fact does not, however, give carte blanche to political realism in the sense that realism's explanatory power with respect to the emergence of the SADC is not without its own difficulties. Realism's focus on the state and power politics as an explanatory variable faces its own limits; it tends to leave out a variety of key variables. Specifically, through its focus on the state, the realist paradigm fails to account for a key variable: individual political leadership. The rise of the SADC shows the essential role that individual leaders can play in the emergence of security communities.

In this respect, Walter Mattli's (1999, 7) contention that many analysts have discarded the role of charismatic leaders as explanatory factors for integration is one which deserves special attention. For Mattli, the reason why individual leaders have been left out of the analysis of international integration is related to the theories' inability to explain the numerous failures of political leaders and the consequences of such failures, which include long phases of stagnation in the process of building international communities. For this particular reason, according to Mattli, the role of political leadership is frequently underanalyzed. The emergence of the SADC and the key role which political leaders such as President Robert Mugabe of Zimbabwe and President Ketumile Masire of Botswana played calls for a revision of such paradigms. Such revision could be all the more legitimate since the cases of the AU, ECOWAS and the SADC seem to signal a pattern, one in which political leaders are front and center in the creation of communities in general and security communities in particular.

VI. Conclusion

The main goal of this chapter was to test three major paradigms of international integration with respect to the emergence of the Southern African Development Community (SADC). The institutional evolution of the SADC bears significant amounts of resemblances to that of ECOWAS and is much different from that of the African Union. Like ECOWAS and contrary to the case of the AU, SADC emerged as an organization primarily centered on economic issues and mutated into a security community in 1992 when the SADCC became the SADC. Like the cases of the African Union and ECOWAS, however, the case of the SADC shows that the traditional paradigms of international politics and international integration in particular do not fully explain the emergence of security communities in the African context. Moreover, as in the cases of the African Union and ECOWAS, realism seems to provide a better explanation for the emergence of the SADC than liberalism and constructivism in the sense that the case of the SADC shows that security communities may also emanate in part from realpolitik.

The liberal hypothesis, which is structured around the idea that shared democratic values is the sine qua non for the rise of security communities has shown its limits in the face of the SADC, a community in which the vast majority of its members do not share in the democratic principle. The constructivist hypothesis, which is built around the idea that shared identities at the elite level are the determinant condition for the rise of security communities, has also shown its limits in the face of a community created on the basis of shared borders. The realist paradigm seems to be more in line with the conditions under which the SADC was created. Such conditions, in the case of the SADC as well as in the case of the AU and ECOWAS, are based on a structural community rather than on a community of values and identity. It is also important to note that although realism seems to provide the most useful explanation for the rise of the SADC as well as the other two African experiments in integration, realism, however, is lacking in its focus on the state as the unit of analysis. In light of all these facts, the three African cases in security integration do call for a new set of hypotheses that would take into account a new set of variables that have been left out by the three major traditional paradigms of international politics.

mainly with followership and processes of interpersonal relations rather than with positions in a hierarchical structure (Edinger 1975). This chapter will examine the question of leadership both in terms of the role of individual political leaders in the creation of communities and security communities as well as the institutional settings within which such leadership evolves. Accordingly, the two major hypotheses that will be generated in this chapter will focus on these two major aspects of political leadership.

Hypothesis 1: Communities are more likely to emerge when a charismatic political leader is willing to be the driving force behind the organization.

The essence of the scholarship on the impact of individual leaders on the rise of communities in general and security communities in particular may be summed up by Cassius' oft-cited admonition to Brutus that the fault lies not in our stars, but in ourselves. In fact, the history of economics, sociology and political science is fraught with debates on the impact of individual leaders on human progress. Such debates reveal a significant amount of divergence as well as convergence among scholars of political leadership. For instance, while Karl Marx (1852) and Leo Tolstoy (1869) argue that leaders can only choose from options that are strictly limited by factors over which they have no control, John Keegan (1998) maintains that the political history of the twentieth century can be written as the biographies of six political leaders: Lenin, Roosevelt, Churchill, Hitler, Stalin and Mao.

Do individual leaders matter? Most specifically, does the behavior of individual political leaders alone matter in the rise of security communities? These questions remain unsettled. For Samuels (2003, 1), "[i]t is obvious that leaders matter." Citing the cases of Bismarck, Churchill, Mandela, Thatcher, Mao and Gandhi, he argues that the behavior of individual leaders and the choices they make take precedence over institutional, historical or any other constraints. For him, leadership is the determining factor in shaping history and historical forces are only secondary to their talents and will. "In short," says Samuels, "constraints may be greater in the historian's narrative than they are in the real world, where social, political and economic forces can be tipped into the balance to abet the leader's scheme" (Samuels 2003, 2). He makes his case by analyzing two countries: Italy and Japan. For him, the fact that these two countries. with strong similarities both structurally and culturally. came to different developmental outcomes is an unmistakable result of the choices of their individual leaders.

There is merit not only in Samuels' argument but in the evidence that he brings forward in support of such argument. It is indeed legitimate to argue in light of historical facts, as he does, that a great number of historical outcomes could be less the products of historical and institutional contexts than they are the result of the choices of different individual leaders. On this account his reference to the above-mentioned historic figures, who have achieved results that would have been different without them, could be quite legitimate. One may also note that Samuels' argument finds support within the intellectual community, especially among those who hold the "Great Man" view. Like

Samuels, Daniel Byman and Kenneth Pollack have aimed to "rescue men and women, as individuals, from the oblivion to which political scientists have consigned them" (Byman and Pollack 2001, 109). In his analysis of the role of individual leaders, Samuels, however, goes a step further in his admonition of political scientists for ignoring the fact that "history is nearly a bottom-less well of resources in the hands of particularly able leaders" (Samuels 2003, 360). It is important to note, to Samuels' credit, that individual leaders have in fact used history and institutions as tools to advance their own agendas. Most importantly, they have also been the creators of history and institutions. Such evidence can be seen, for instance, in his argument regarding why corporatism succeeded in Japan and yet failed in Italy under two different types of leader-ship that varied in quality (Samuels 2003, 151).

In the case of Africa, such evidence could be seen in the fact that the AU, ECOWAS and the SADC emerged in spite of the absence of the conventional pre-requisites, including shared values and identities at the elite level—prerequisites dear to both the liberal and constructivist paradigms. To the contrary, the emergence of these three communities may be more a function of one essential dimension of leadership—statecraft—which is the ability of a leader to steer the political system toward outcomes that accord with their goals (Rockman 1984, 11). Such ability, according to Jackson and Rosberg, could be more ac-centuated in the African case than it is in the European case in the absence of strong constraining domestic institutions in Africa. Jackson and Rosberg explain further, "It is apparent from the historical evidence that African rulers and other leaders are not captives of their environments" (Jackson and Rosberg 1982, 3). For the authors, such importance of individual leaders can also be measured in terms the successes and failures of individual African leaders to provide such political goods as peace, order, stability and nonmaterial security.

Thus, the argument relative to the impact of individual political leaders on the rise and functioning of international communities in general and security communities in particular is not without merit. Nowhere are such merits more obvious than in the ways in which all three communities emerged not only as general communities but also, and most importantly, as security communities. The rise of all three communities, as we have shown in the preceding chapters, was largely driven by the will and resolve of particular individual leaders who managed to get other African leaders aboard. One of the most crucial illustra-tions to this point can be seen in the story of ECOWAS.

The story of the West African community is marked by a leadership struggle of the first order; a struggle in which two different kinds of leadership were entrenched in two different camps: Francophone leaders versus Anglophone leaders. The existence of these two camps with two different political philoso-phies almost aborted the birth of a security community but for the resolve of one individual leader. In their analysis of the emergence of ECOMOG, which established ECOWAS as a security community, most scholars contend that the decision to create ECOMOG in the height of the Liberian civil war was depicted by Francophone West African leaders as a move by the Anglophone section of the organization (Francis 2001).

Consequently, in a gesture of retaliation, and for personal motivations and interests, Blaise Compaore of Burkina Faso and Houphouët-Boigny of Côte d'Ivoire (both French speaking leaders and members of ECOWAS) opposed the creation of ECOMOG. ECOMOG emerged, however, despite fierce opposition from Francophone West African leaders mainly because of the resolve of President Babangida of Nigeria. He managed to set up a peacekeeping force consisting mainly of troops from three Anglophone West African states (Nigeria, Ghana and Sierra Leone) along with one Francophone State (Guinea, which has historically been the outcast of the Francophone group).

Despite its inherent strength, however, the argument relative to the impact of individual leaders on the rise of security communities faces its own limits. One such limit may rest with the scholarship's view of the weight of historical factors in comparison to the individual forces that the political leaders represent. In other words, the scholarship's fault may lie not in its recognition of the importance of individual leaders per se, but in the weight it accords individual leaders. Such a weight seems bigger in the scholarship's accounts than individual leaders may actually possess. In politics, as in history in general, one has to reckon with the broader dynamics of history (what Samuels (2003, 1) calls "large and impersonal forces"). Thus, Samuels' contention that, instead of constituting constraints, these larger and impersonal forces could be just other factors that the leader may incorporate in his scheme may be a bit simplistic. In fact, some of these impersonal forces do determine and have often determined whether some leaders will ever be in a position to exert any type of influence in the first place.

As a matter of fact, one could not find better examples than the ones that Samuels chooses to study in order to make a legitimate case for the importance of impersonal forces not as mere subordinates to leaders but as forces capable of dictating outcomes in themselves. All the leaders that he dwelt on, from Count Cavour to Ishihara Shintaro, creative and powerful as they may have been, operated within a certain historical and institutional framework that were beyond their control. The mere fact that most of these leaders came to power obeys, in fact, a certain historical and institutional logic. Men certainly make history and institutions but they may not necessarily exercise control over historical and institutional realities once they are created. In the African case, one could legitimately argue that Khaddafi, Mbeki, Obasanjo, Eyadéma, Gowon or Mugabe were able to rise to power and follow a certain course of action, which resulted in the emergence of Africa's three major communities, only because the existing institutional arrangements at that particular time in history allowed them such possibilities. In sum, although the idea that political leaders are complete prisoners of their institutional environments may be a bit of an exaggeration, the notion that institutional factors may play a role in the leadership's ability to shape a variety of outcomes (including the emergence of communities) is not. For this reason, Hypothesis 2 will focus on the institutional setting as an explanatory variable for the impact of political leadership on the rise of security communities in Africa.

Hypothesis 2: Communities are more likely to emerge when a charismatic political leader is willing to be the driving force behind the organization in the presence of favorable institutional factors.

One of the most important lessons which could be derived from the testing of Hypothesis 1 is that although individual leaders do matter, the question of the impact of individual leadership on the emergence of communities and security communities also has to be analyzed within the institutional context in which such leadership operates. Most specifically, it has to be analyzed in terms of the relationship between the leadership and such political institutions. Although political institutions are products of the leadership, the rapport between the two constitutes a determining factor in shaping outcomes. This is all the more legitimate since in the case of Africa, as well as in the case of most Third World countries, there is an inverse relationship between the strength of political leadership and the strength of political institutions. In other words, the stronger the leadership, the weaker the institutions within which they evolve (Jackson and Rosberg 1982).

This dynamic is built from the Weberian notion that leaders matter most when institutions matter least. The weakness of such institutions encourages the emergence of personal leadership. The cycle is maintained by the fact that these personalistic leaders participate in turn in the weakening of the already weak institutions. According to Jackson and Rosberg, "African politics are most often a personal or factional struggle ... that is restrained by private and tacit agreements, prudential concerns and personal ties and dependencies rather than by public rules and institutions" (Jackson and Rosberg 1982, 1).

To be sure, the role of strong individual leaders in the creation of international and domestic institutions for that matter is not an exclusively African phenomenon. In fact, historically, the political institutions that are associated today with the modern state are the products of powerful and personal rulers (Jackson and Rosberg 1982, 5). Europe constitutes the prime illustration of this point. However, in the case of Europe, such personal rule in general corresponded to a transition period, whereas in the case of Africa, such transition seems endless, as various forms of personal political struggles and conflicts at the highest levels continue to dominate political life. This fact makes the analysis of the African experiment in integration through the contributions of its individual leaders all the more legitimate. Jackson and Rosberg's (1982, 266) argument that Machiavelli and Hobbes are more useful than the "constitutions" for understanding the characteristics and dynamics of African politics could be understood in such light.

The underlying question which Jackson and Rosberg's remark raises, however, is, how could the emergence of communities in general and security communities in particular be explained as the result of the interplay between individual leaders and the institutional context within which they operate? Such a question can be tackled by examining the dynamics of the relationship between institutional design and individual leadership.

Transformational leaders—leaders who drive the creation of communities in general and security communities in particular—most often benefit from the existence of a strong state institutional apparatus. In most cases, such individual leaders are backed by states with a strong economic and military apparatus. But the backing of a strong economic and military apparatus is not, however, always a necessary condition. The AU was driven by leaders with the backing of states with strong economic apparatus (South Africa, Nigeria) as well as by states with medium economic and military power (Libya) and states with less strong economic and military power (Algeria and Senegal). In addition, the key role of Eyadéma of Togo in the creation of ECOWAS may also reinforce this point. In all of these cases, the constant is individual leadership.

Such leadership has been shown in the case of the emergence of the AU with Khaddafi as well as in the case of the OAU with Kwame Nkrumah. Such leadership is also clear in the case of ECOWAS as a general community with Eyadéma and Gowon as well as in the role of Babangida in the transformation of ECOWAS from a mainly political and economic community into a security community in 1990 with the rise of ECOMOG. Finally, such leadership is also demonstrably clear with Mugabe's role both in the emergence of the SADCC and in the transformation of the SADCC into the SADC, which marked the organization's transmutation into a security community. Moreover, such importance of leadership is made clear in the key roles of Nyerere of Tanzania and Kaunda of Zambia in the creation and functioning of the FLS, which evolved into a more formal framework for security integration in southern Africa.

Maxi Schoeman's (2002) argument that politics, rather than economic considerations, has determined the establishment and functioning of the SADCC (1980–1993) and thereafter of the SADC (from 1993) and that these politics-driven processes have significant impacts on the development of the southern African region could be understood in such light. In other words, the emergence of the SADCC and the SADC must not only be understood in terms of economic imperatives but, most importantly, in terms of the will and motivations of political leaders.

Chapter 8

Conclusion

This study has sought to test three major paradigms of international politics—liberalism, constructivism and realism—in light of the emergence of three major African communities—the African Union (AU), the Economic Community of West African States (ECOWAS) and the Southern African Development Community (SADC). Our findings suggest that none of the three paradigms explains satisfactorily the emergence of Africa's three communities.

Interestingly, however, the emergence of Africa's three communities is better grasped by the realist paradigm than by the liberal or constructivist paradigm; the history of the AU, ECOWAS and the SADC is more about structure and interest than it is about values and identities. Our research has also uncovered the significant role that leadership has played in building Africa's three communities. In this sense, the realist paradigm, in turn, comes short in its explanation. Realism's focus on the state as the unit of analysis is problematic because, as we demonstrated, it tends to either leave out this key variable of individual leadership or to conflate the state and individual leadership.

The history of the emergence of Africa's communities is not only about the state, structure and interest; it is also about the actions of individual political leaders. The emergence of Africa's three communities was dictated by the resolve of singular individual African leaders. Such resolve, as we have shown in the preceding lines, can be seen in the crucial roles of Khaddafi in the emergence of the AU, Eyadéma and Gowon in the rise of ECOWAS, Babangida in the rise of ECOMOG and Mugabe in the development of both the SADCC and the SADC. Such leadership preponderance was equally manifest during Africa's earliest attempts in international community building in the aftermath of the birth of most African modern states in the 1960s. Specifically, such tradition in leadership preponderance could be traced back to the overriding roles of leaders such as Kwame Nkrumah in the creation the OAU, the forerunner of the AU, as well as to the key roles of Julius Nyerere and Kenneth Kaunda in the emergence of the FLS, the forerunner of the SADCC and the SADC.

The theoretical underpinnings of leadership preponderance can be located at the nexus of the relationship between leadership and institutions. As we have argued previously, such leadership tends to be unusually preponderant in Africa in the absence of strong institutional constraints. In this sense, the findings of this study strengthen the growing arguments that focusing on individual leaders instead of focusing on states as the units of analysis may better illuminate the international phenomena (Wolford 2007).

It is important, however, to point out that such arguments do not specifically focus on the role of individual leaders in the emergence of security communities. As a matter of fact, the bulk of the scholarship focuses generally on conflict resolution (Morrow 1989; Press 2005; Wolford 2007) and economic performance (Hall and Jones 1999; Jones and Olken 2005; Olson 1993; Olsen 2000). In the same vein, this study has attempted to expand such arguments on the centrality of individual leaders in the creation of communities and security communities.

Do leaders matter? Our findings suggest that they do and that they are not incidental to the rise of communities and security communities in Africa's. Africa's political leaders, however, like leaders in general, do not exist in a vacuum. They are also the products of institutional environments. Thus, the emergence of communities in general and security communities in particular in Africa is a product of the interaction between its leadership and the institutional environment within which they evolve. The preceding lines, by showing that the rise of communities in Africa is to a great extent a function of its leadership in relation to the institutional environment within which it operates, reinforce such notion. Such leadership, however, as we have shown in Chapter 7, has been able to transcend the institutional settings of its respective states in its quest for international institution building.

In this sense, it is also important to note that despite the influence of institutional factors on Africa's leaders, such leaders do hold a central place in the creation of communities and security communities in Africa. In the same vein, while our findings recognize the centrality of Deutsch's arguments, they depart from them in significant ways. Deutsch argues that elites are important but that they are important only to the extent that his three major conditions—shared values and expectations, capabilities and communication processes and mutual predictability of behavior—are met. The cases of the three African communities show that leadership can engineer a community even in the absence of such primary conditions. In this sense, the history of Africa is the history of its leadership writ large.

References

Addona, A. F. 1969. *The Organization of African Unity*. Cleveland: World Pub. Co.

Adler, Emmanuel, and Michael Barnett. 1998. "Security Communities in Theoretical Perspectives." In *Security Communities*, edited by Emmanuel Adler and Michael Barnett. Cambridge: Cambridge University Press.

Annan, Koffi. 2004. "Address to the African Union Summit." Addis Ababa, Ethiopia. Available online at the UN's website at http://www.un.org/apps/sg/sgstats.asp?nid=1012. Accessed June 30, 2014.

Bah, Alhaji. 2005. "West Africa: From a Security Complex to a Security Community." *African Security Review* 14(2): 1–4.

Braeckman, Colette. 1999. "Carve-up in the Congo." *Le Monde Diplomatique,* available online in English at http://mondediplo.com/1999/10/08congo. Accessed June 30, 2014.

Bury, J. B, and Russell Meiggs. 1975. *A History of Greece to the Death of Alexander the Great*, Fourth Edition. New York: St. Martin's Press.

Byman, Daniel L., and Kenneth M. Pollack. 2001. "Let Us Now Praise Great Men: Bringing the Statesman Back In." *International Security* 25 (4): 107–146.

Carr, E. H. 1939. *The Twenty Years' Crisis, 1919–1939*. New York: Harper Collins Publishers.

Cawthra, Gavin. 1997. "Sub-Regional Security Cooperation: The Southern African Development Community in Comparative Perspective." Belville: The Copenhagen Peace Research Institute: 1-35. Available online at: http://www.ciaonet.org/wps/cag01. Accessed October 30, 2008.

Checkel, Jeffrey. 2001. "Why Comply? Social Learning and European Identity Change." *International Organization* 55 (3): 553–588.

Ching'ambo, L. J. 1992. "Towards a Defence Alliance in Southern Africa?" *Southern Africa Political and Economic Monthly* 5 (8): 36–38.

Cilliers, Jakkie. 1999. "The Legacy of the Front-line States." Published in Monograph No 43: Building Security in Southern Africa. Available online at http://www.iss.co.za/Pubs/Monographs/No43/TheLegacy. html#Anchor-7905. Accessed October 30, 2008.

Cisse, Youssouf Tata. 2003. La charte du Mandé et autres traditions du Mali. Paris: Albin Michel.

Clapham, Christopher. 2001. "The Changing World of Regional Integration in Africa." In *Regional Integration in Southern Africa: Comparative International Perspectives* edited by C. Clapham, G. Mills, A. Morner and E. Sidiropoulos. South African Institute of International Affairs.

Cohen, Ronald. 1967. *The Kanuri of Bornu.* New York: Holt, Rinehart and Winston, Inc.

Collier, Paul, and Terry Venables. 2008. "Trade and Economic Performance: Does Africa's Fragmentation Matter?" Annual World Bank Conference on Development Economics, Cape Town, South Africa, June.

Conteh-Morgan, Earl. 1993. "ECOWAS: Peace-Making or Meddling in Liberia?" *Africa Insight* 23(1): 36–41.

____. 1998. "Introduction: Adapting Peace-Making Mechanisms in a Era of Global Change." In *Peacekeeping in Africa*, edited by Karl P. Magyar and Earl Conteh-Morgan. New York: St. Martin Press, Inc., 1–11.

Cooley, William D. 1966. *The Negroland of the Arabs Examined and Explained.* London: Routledge.

Curtin, Phillip. 1995. "Africa North of the Forest in the Early Islamic Age." In *African History from Earliest Times to Independence,* Second Edition, edited by Phillip Curtin, Steven Feierman, Leonard Thompson and Jan Vansina. New York: Longman Publishing, 64–98.

Deng, Francis M., and I. William Zartman. 2002. *A Strategic Vision for Africa: The Kampala Movement.* Washington, DC: Brookings Institution Press.

Deutsch, Karl W. 1954. *Political Community at the International Level: Problems of Definition and Measurement.* Garden City: Doubleday & Company, Inc.

Deutsch, Karl W., Sidney A. Burrell, Robert A. Kann, Maurice Lee Jr., Martin Lichterman, Raymond E. Lindgren, Francis L. Loewheim and Richard W. Van Wagenen. 1957. *Political Community and the North Atlantic Area.* Princeton: Princeton University Press.

Diop, Cheikh A. 1987. *Black Africa: The Economic and Cultural Basis for a Federated State.* Trenton, NJ: Africa World Press. Translated from the French by Harold J. Salemson.

Doyle, Michael. 1997. *The Ways of War and Peace*. New York: Norton.

Edinger, Lewis J. 1975. "The Comparative Analysis of Political Leadership." *Comparative Politics* 7 (2): 253–269.

Ero, Comfort. 2000. "ECOMOG: A Model for Africa?" Published in Monograph 46, Building Stability in Africa: Challenges for the New Millennium, February 2000:1–9.

Etzioni, Amitae. 1965. *Political Unification*. New York: Holt, Rinehart and Winston.

Ewi, Martin, and Kwesi Aning. 2006. "Assessing the Role of the African Union in Preventing and Combating Terrorism in Africa." *African Security Review* 15(3): 32–46.

Fage, J. D. 1995. *A History of Africa,* Third Edition. New York: Routledge.

Fage, J. D., and Roland Anthony Oliver. 1975. *The Cambridge History of Africa*. Cambridge: The Cambridge University Press.

Farber, Henry S., and Joanne Gowa. 1997. "Common Interests or Common Polities? Reinterpreting the Democratic Peace." *The Journal of Politics* 59 (2): 393–417.

Francis, David J. 2001. "Post-Adjustment, Regional Integration and Human Security in Africa." In *Politics and Economics of Africa*, edited by Frank Columbus. New York: Nova Science Publishers, Inc., 1–15.

Franke, Benedikt. 2008. "Africa's Evolving Security Architecture and the Concept of Multilayered Security Communities." *Cooperation and Conflict* 43 (3): 313–340.

Friedman, Milton. 1953. *Essays in Positive Economics*. Chicago: University of Chicago Press.

Galtung, Johan. 1968. "A Structural Theory of Integration." *Journal of Peace Research* 5 (4): 375–395.

Gilpin, Robert. 1987. *The Political Economy of International Relations*. Princeton, NJ: Princeton University Press.

Gompert, David C. 2006. "For a Capability to Protect: Mass Killing, the African Union and NATO." *Survival* 48 (1): 7–17.

Haas, Ernest B. 1958. *The Uniting of Europe: Political, Social and Economic Forces 1950–1957*. Stanford: Stanford University Press.

____. 1961. "International Integration: The European and the Universal Process." *International Organization* 15 (3): 366–392.

____. 1975. "The Obsolescence of Regional Integration Theory." Research Studies 25, Institute of International Studies, Berkeley, CA.

Hall, Robert E., and Charles I. Jones. 1999. "Why Do Some Countries Produce So Much More Output per Worker Than Others?" *Quarterly Journal of Economics* 114 (1): 83–116.

Hardin, Garrett. 1968. "The Tragedy of the Commons." *Science* 162: 1243–1248.

Herz, John H. 1951. *Political Realism and Political Idealism*. Chicago: University of Chicago Press.

Hobbes, Thomas. [1651] 1991. *Leviathan*. Cambridge: Cambridge University Press.

Hopf, Ted. 2002. *Social Construction of International Politics: Identities and Foreign Policies, Moscow, 1955 and 1999*. Ithaca: Cornell University Press.

Howard, Michael. 1978. *War and the Liberal Conscience*. New Brunswick: Rutgers University Press.

Huntzinger, Jacques. 1977. *Europes* [French]. Paris: Ramsay.

____. 1987. Introduction aux Relations Internationales. Paris: Editions du Seuil.

Jackson, Robert H., and Carl G. Rosberg. 1982. *Personal Rule in Black Africa*. Berkeley: University of California Press.

Jepperson, Ronald, Alexander Wendt and Peter Katzenstein. 1996. "Norms, Identity and Culture in National Security." In *The Culture of National Security: Norms and Identity in World Politics*, edited by Peter Katzenstein. New York: Columbia University Press, 33–75.

Jervis, Robert. 1978. "Cooperation Under the Security Dilemma." *World Politics* 30 (2): 167–214.

Jones, Benjamin F., and Benjamin A. Olken. 2005. "Do Leaders Matter? National Leadership and Growth since World War II." *The Quarterly Journal of Economics* 120 (3): 835–864.

Kant, Immanuel. 1795. "Perpetual Peace." In *Kant Political Writings*. Reprinted by H. Reiss. 1992. Cambridge: Cambridge University Press, 93–131.

Katzenstein, Peter. 1996. *The Culture of National Security: Norms and Identity in World Politics*. New York: Columbia University Press.

Keck, Margaret, and Kathryn Sikkink. 1998. *Activists Beyond Borders: Advocacy Networks in International Politics*. Ithaca: Cornell University Press.

Keegan, John. 1998. "Winston Churchill." *Time Magazine*, April, 151: 114–117.

Keohane, Robert. 1986. "Realism, Neorealism and the Study of World Politics." In *Neorealism and its Critics*, edited by Robert Keohane. New York: Columbia University Press.

____. 1989. *International Institutions and State Power: Essays in International Relations Theory*. Boulder, CO: Westview Press.

Keohane, Robert, and Joseph Nye. 2001. *Power and Interdependence,* Third Edition. Harrisonburg: R. R. Donnelley & Sons Company.

Khobe, Maxwell. 2000. "The Evolution and Conduct of ECOMOG Operations in West Africa". Published in Monograph No 44: Boundaries of Peace Support Operations. Available online at http://www.iss.co.za/Pubs/Monographs/No44/ECOMOG.html. Accessed June 20, 2014.

Kindleberger, Charles P. 1986. *The World in Depression, 1929–1939*. Berkeley: University of California Press.

Ki-Zerbo, Joseph. 1978. *Histoire de L'Afrique Noire: D'hier a Demain*. Paris: Hatier.

Kratochwil, Friedrich. 1989. *Rules, Norms and Decisions*. Cambridge: Cambridge University Press.

Legro, Jeffrey W. 2005. *Rethinking the World: Great Power Strategies and International Order*. Ithaca, NY: Cornell University Press.

Lindberg, Leon. 1963. *The Political Dynamics of European Economic Integration*. Stanford: Stanford University Press.

Machiavelli, Niccolo. [1513] 1992. *The Prince*. New York: Alfred A. Knopf.

March, James, and Johan Olsen. 1998. "The Institutional Dynamics of International Political Orders." International Organization 52 (4): 943–969.

Marx, Karl. 1852. "The Eighteenth Brumaire of Louis Napoleon." Die Revolution: New York.

Mattli, Walter. 1999. *The Logic of Regional Integration: Europe and Beyond*. Cambridge: Cambridge University Press.

Mbeki, Thabo. 2002. "Speech at the Launch of the African Union." Durban, South Africa. Available online at the website of South Africa's Department of Foreign Affairs at http://www.dfa.gov.za/docs/speeches/2002/mbek0709.htm. Accessed October 30, 2008.

Mearsheimer, John J. 1990. "Back to the Future: Instability in Europe After the Cold War." *International Security* 15 (1): 5–56.

____. 1994/1995. "The False Promise of International Institutions." *International Security* 19(3): 5–49.

____. 2001. *The Tragedy of Great Power Politics*. New York: Norton.

Miller, Benjamin. 2005. "When and How Regions Become Peaceful: Potential Theoretical Pathways to Peace." *International Studies Review* 7 (2): 229–267.

Mitrany, David. 1975. *The Functional Theory of Politics*. London: Martin Robertson.

Momoh, Abubakar. 2000. "The Security Imperatives of the Crises in West Africa: Preliminary Thoughts." Monograph No. 50, Franco-South African Dialogue Sustainable Security in Africa, compiled by Diane Philander. Available online at: http://www.iss.co.za/Pubs/Monographs/No50/Chap10. html. Accessed June 30, 2014.

Morgenthau, Hans J. 1946. *Scientific Man versus Power Politics*. Chicago: University of Chicago Press.

____. 1951. *In Defense of the National Interest: A Critical Examination of American Foreign Policy*. New York: Alfred A. Knopf.

____. [1948] 1973. *Politics Among Nations: The Struggle for Power and Peace*. New York: Alfred A. Knopf.

Morrow, James. 1989. "Capabilities, Uncertainty, and Resolve: A Limited Information Model of Crisis Bargaining." *American Journal of Political Science* 33 (4): 941–972.

Mortimer, Robert A. 1996. "ECOMOG, Liberia, and Regional Security in West Africa." In *Africa in the New International Order: Rethinking State Sovereignty and Regional Security*, edited by Edmond Keller and Donald Rothchild. Boulder, CO: Lynne Rienner Publishers, 149–164.

Ngoma, Naison. 2005. *Prospects for a Security Community in the Southern African Context: An Analysis of Regional Security in the Southern African Development Community*. Pretoria: Institute for Security Studies.

Nivet, Sebastien. 2006. *Security by Proxy? The EU and (sub) Regional Organizations: The Case of ECOWAS*. Paris: Institute for Security Studies.

Nkrumah, Kwame. 1963. *Africa Must Unite*. New York: Frederick A. Praeger, Inc.

Nye, Joseph. 1965. *Pan-Africanism and East African Integration*. Cambridge: Harvard University Press.

Oakley, Robin. 2001. "OAU's Questionable Purpose and Prospects," CNN World. Available online at: http://edition.cnn.com/2001/WORLD/africa/07/09/ africa.oau July 9, 2001. Accessed June 15, 2014.

Olson, Mancur. 1993. "Dictatorship, Democracy, and Development." American Political Science Review 87 (3): 567–576.

Onuf, Nicholas. 1989. *A World of Our Making*. Columbia: University of South Carolina Press.

Oosthuizen, Gabriël. 2006. *The Southern African Development Community: The Organisation, its History, Policies and Prospects*. Midrand: The Institute for Global Dialogue.

Owen, John. 1994. "How Liberalism Produces Democratic Peace." *International Security* 19 (2): 87–125.

Press, Daryl. 2005. *Calculating Credibility: How Leaders Assess Military Threats.* Ithaca: Cornell University Press.

Ripsman, Norrin M. 2005. "Two Stages of Transition from a Region of War to a Region of Peace: Realist Transition and Liberal Endurance." *International Studies* Quarterly 49 (4): 669–693.

Risse-Kappen, Thomas. 1996. "Collective Identity in a Democratic Community: The Case of NATO." In *The Culture of National Security: Norms and Identity in World Politics*, edited by Peter Katzenstein. New York: Columbia University Press, 357–399.

Rockman, Bert. 1984. *The Leadership Question.* New York: Praeger.

Rosamond, Ben. 2000. *Theories of European Integration.* New York: St. Martin's Press.

Rosenau, James N. 1992. "Citizenship in a Changing Global Order." In *Governance Without Government: Order and Change in World Politics*, edited by James Rosenau and Ernst-Otto Czempiel. New York: Cambridge University Press, 272–294.

Rousseau, Jean J. 1755. *Discourse upon the Origin and the Foundation of the Inequality among Mankind.* Translated by Franklin Philip. Edited with an introduction by Patrick Coleman. 1994. New York: Oxford University Press.

____. 1761. "A Project for Perpetual Peace." Translated from the French, with a preface by the translator. London, 1–48.

Ruggie, John. 1998. *Constructing the World Polity: Essays on International Institutionalization.* New York: Routledge.

Russett, Bruce. 1993. *Grasping the Democratic Peace: Principles for a Post–Cold War World.* Princeton: Princeton University Press.

Samuels, Richard J. 2003. *Machiavelli's Children: Leaders and Their Legacies in Italy and Japan.* Ithaca: Cornell University Press.

Sarr, Mamadou. 1991. *The Empire of Mali.* Bamako: M.E.N.

Schalkwyk, Gina. 2005. "SADC: Creating a Security Community for Southern Africa?" Presented at the Institute for Security Studies. Pretoria, South Africa.

Schoeman, Maxi. 2002. "Imagining a Community: The African Union as an Emerging Security Community." *Strategic Review for Southern Africa* 24 (1): 1–26.

Schumpeter, Joseph. [1951] 1965. *Imperialism and Social Classes: Two Essays.* Cleveland: World Publishing Company.

Sideway, James, and Richard Gibb. 1998. "SADC, COMESA, SACU: Contradictory Formats for Regional 'Integration' in Southern Africa?" In

South Africa in Southern Africa: Reconfiguring the Region, edited by David Simon. Athens, OH: Ohio University Press, 164–184.

Skocpol, Theda. 1979. *States and Social Revolutions*. New York: Cambridge University Press.

Skocpol, Theda, and Margaret Somers. 1980. "The Use of Comparative History in Macro-Sociological Inquiry." *Comparative Studies in Society and History* 22 (2):174–197.

Smith, Steve. 1987. "Paradigm Dominance in International Relations: The Development of International Relations as a Social Science." *Journal of International Studies* 16 (2): 189–204.

Spero, Joan, and Jeffrey Hart. 1997. *The Politics of International Economics*, Fifth Edition. New York: St. Martin's Press.

Spiro, David. 1994. "The Insignificance of the Liberal Peace." *International Security* 19 (2): 50–86.

Stride, G. T., and Caroline Ifeka. 1971. *Peoples and Empires of West Africa: West Africa in History, 1000–1800*. New York: Africana Publishing Corporation.

Suberu Rotimi T. 2005. "Renovating the Architecture of Federalism in Nigeria: The Option of Non-Constitutional Renewal." Paper Prepared by Panel Participants for the Conference on "Aid, Governance and Development in Africa" held May 12–14, 2005, at Northwestern University. Available online at http://www.northwestern.edu/african-studies/AGDpapers.html. Accessed July 15, 2015.

Talentino, Andrea. 2005. *Military Intervention After the Cold War*. Athens, OH: Ohio University Press.

Thomas, Daniel C. 2001. *The Helsinki Effect: International Norms, Human Rights, and the Demise of Communism*. Princeton: Princeton University Press.

Thucydides. [431 BC] 1972. *History of the Peloponnesian War*. New York: Penguin Books.

Tolstoy, Leo. 1938. *War and Peace*. Translated from the Russian by Louise and Aylmer Maude. New York: The Heritage Press.

Tschiyembe, Mwayila. 1999. "Africa's New Players Jostle for Power." *Le Monde diplomatique*, available online in English at http://mondediplo.com/1999/01/18africa. Accessed June 13, 2014.

UNECA. 2006. "Assessing Regional Integration in Africa II: Rationalizing Regional Economic Communities." United Nations Economic Commission for Africa and African Union, Addis Ababa. Available online at: http://www.uneca.org/aria. Accessed July 17, 2015.

Van de Walle, Nicholas. 2005. "The Stagnant Low-Income States." In *Overcoming Stagnation in Aid-Dependent Countries*. Washington, DC: Center for Global Development, 7–36.

Van Evera, Stephen. 1997. *Guide to Methods for Students of Political Science*. Ithaca: Cornell University Press.

Venter, Denis. 1996. "Regional Security in Southern Africa in the Post–Cold War Era." In *Africa in the New International Order*, edited by Edmond Keller and Donald Rothchild. Boulder, CO: Lynne Rienner Publishers, 134–148.

Vogt, Margaret A. 1996. "The Involvement of ECOWAS in Liberia's Peacekeeping." In *Africa in the New International Order: Rethinking State Sovereignty and Regional Security*, edited by Edmond J. Keller and Donald Rothchild. Boulder, CO: Lynne Rienner Publishers, 165–183.

Wallander, Celeste A. 2000. "Institutional Assets and Adaptability: NATO after the Cold War." *International Organization* 54 (4): 705–735.

Waltz, Kenneth. 1979. *Theory of International Politics*. Reading, MA: Addison-Wesley.

____. 1986a. "Anarchic Orders and Balances of Power." In *Neorealism and its Critics*, edited by Robert Keohane. New York: Columbia University Press, 98–130.

____. 1986b. "Reflections on Theory of International Politics: A Response to My Critics." In *Neorealism and its Critics*, edited by Robert Keohane. New York: Columbia University Press, 322–345.

Weber, Cynthia. 2001. *International Relations Theory: A Critical Introduction*. New York: Routledge.

Wendt, Alexander. 1992. "Anarchy Is What States Make of It: The Social Construction of Power Politics." *International Organization* 46 (2): 391–425.

____. 1994. "Collective Identity Formation and the International State." *American Political Science Review* 88 (2): 384–396.

____. 1999. *Social Theory of International Politics*. Cambridge: Cambridge University Press.

Williams, Michael C. 2001. "The Discipline of the Democratic Peace: Kant, Liberalism and the Social Construction of Security Communities." *European Journal of International Relations* 7 (4): 525–553.

____. 2005. *The Realist Tradition and the Limits of International Relations*. Cambridge, UK: Cambridge University Press.

Wolford, Scott. 2007. "The Turnover Trap: New Leaders, Reputation, and International Conflict." *American Journal of Political Science* 51 (4): 772–788.

CPSIA information can be obtained
at www.ICGtesting.com
Printed in the USA
FSOW03n1712271216
28926FS